# THE INDONESIAN KITCHEN

Classic dishes made easy with
over 80 step-by-step recipes

# THE INDONESIAN KITCHEN

Classic dishes made easy with
over 80 step-by-step recipes

Features sensational and authentic dishes for all occasions, shown in
more than 450 mouthwatering photographs Ghillie Başan and Terry Tan

southwater

This edition is published by Southwater,
an imprint of Anness Publishing Ltd,
Blaby Road, Wigston, Leicestershire LE18 4SE

Email: info@anness.com

Web: www.southwaterbooks.com; www.annesspublishing.com

If you like the images in this book and would like to investigate using
them for publishing, promotions or advertising, please visit our website
www.practicalpictures.com for more information.

Publisher: Joanna Lorenz
Editorial Director: Helen Sudell
Editors: Emma Clegg, Rosie Gordon and Elizabeth Young
Contributing Editors: Beverley Jollands and Alison Bolus
Page Design: Ian Sandom
Cover Design: Sarah Rock
Home Economists: Lucy McKelvie and Katie Giovanni
Photographers: William Lingwood and Martin Brigdale
Stylist: Helen Trent
Production Controller: Bessie Bai

© Anness Publishing Ltd 2011

Previously published as part of a larger volume,
*The Cooking of Indonesia and the Philippines*

Picture Credits
The publisher is grateful to the following for permission to publish
photographs: Alamy pp.10bl, 13b, 16tr, 16bl; Photoshot pp. 11br, 12b,
26b; Travel_ink pp. 6tl, 8tr, 8bl, 9tl, 9br, 11tr, 12t.

Publisher's Notes
Although the advice and information in this book are believed to be
accurate and true at the time of going to press, neither the authors
nor the publisher can accept any legal responsibility or liability for any
errors or omissions that may have been made nor for any inaccuracies
nor for any loss, harm or injury that comes about from following
instructions or advice in this book.

Main front cover image shows Indonesian Chicken Broth – for recipe,
see page 66.

Ethical Trading Policy
At Anness Publishing we believe that business should be conducted
in an ethical and ecologically sustainable way, with respect for the
environment and a proper regard to the replacement of the natural
resources we employ.

As a publisher, we use a lot of wood pulp in high-quality paper for
printing, and that wood commonly comes from spruce trees. We are
therefore currently growing more than 750,000 trees in three Scottish
forest plantations: Berrymoss (130 hectares/320 acres), West Touxhill
(125 hectares/305 acres) and Deveron Forest (75 hectares/185
acres). The forests we manage contain more than 3.5 times the
number of trees employed each year in making paper for the books
we manufacture.

Because of this ongoing ecological investment programme, you, as
our customer, can have the pleasure and reassurance of knowing that
a tree is being cultivated on your behalf to naturally replace the
materials used to make the book you are holding.

Our forestry programme is run in accordance with the UK Woodland
Assurance Scheme (UKWAS) and will be certified by the
internationally recognized Forest Stewardship Council (FSC). The FSC
is a non-government organization dedicated to promoting responsible
management of the world's forests. Certification ensures forests are
managed in an environmentally sustainable and socially responsible
way. For further information about this scheme, go to
www.annesspublishing.com/trees

Notes
For all recipes, quantities are given in both metric and imperial
measures and, where appropriate, in standard cups and spoons.
Follow one set of measures, but not a mixture, because they are
not interchangeable.

Standard spoon and cup measures are level.
1 tsp = 5ml, 1 tbsp = 15ml, 1 cup = 250ml/8fl oz.

Australian standard tablespoons are 20ml. Australian readers
should use 3 tsp in place of 1 tbsp for measuring small quantities.

American pints are 16fl oz/2 cups. American readers should
use 20fl oz/2.5 cups in place of 1 pint when measuring liquids.

Electric oven temperatures in this book are for conventional ovens.
When using a fan oven, the temperature will probably need to be
reduced by about 10–20°C/20–40°F. Since ovens vary, you should
check with your manufacturer's instruction book for guidance.

The nutritional analysis given for each recipe is calculated per
portion (i.e. serving or item), unless otherwise stated. If the recipe
gives a range, such as Serves 4–6, then the nutritional analysis
will be for the smaller portion size, i.e. 6 servings. Measurements
for sodium do not include salt added to taste.

Medium (US large) eggs are used unless otherwise stated.

# CONTENTS

# INTRODUCTION

The food of Indonesia offers a variety of sensational and flavoursome delights. Blending spices and seasonings is an art that has evolved through centuries of multiculturalism, and is integral to the cooking of Indonesia today. The country's history has enriched the cuisine with the addition of exotic spices and new and exciting cooking methods from India, Persia (now Iran) and China.

*Below: A typical Javanese village with thatched houses on stilts, surrounded by paddy fields.*

You will, no doubt, notice some similarities between the dishes in this book. However, whether it has high-octane chilli fire or subtle Chinese savoury characteristics, each dish is memorable for the judicious, and often brilliantly inspired, mixture of ingredients that creates its unique character.

## THE ISLANDS OF INDONESIA

Indonesia's more than 17,000 islands of varying sizes, not all of which have names, are sometimes likened to 'a jewelled necklace'. They lie between Australia and the South-east Asian mainland, and the country includes Java, Bali, Sumatra, parts of Borneo and parts of New Guinea. Fewer than 1,000 of the islands are populated, as some are too small or too barren to support successful habitation.

A total of 234 million residents ranks Indonesia's population as the sixth largest in the world. However, the distribution of people is very uneven, and one third of the total population of the entire archipelago lives in the city of Jakarta – over 80 million people.

The Indonesian landscape and climate have a significant influence on the food. The islands often suffer from floods and volcanic eruptions, which together produce very fertile soil and a lush green landscape. High humidity makes living there a hot and steamy experience, somewhat akin to being in a greenhouse, although the cooler mountain peaks and high volcanic craters running down the backs of most of the major islands provide a welcome relief from these conditions.

The topographical variety leads to the cultivation of many different crops. Rice grows on neatly carved hillside terraces in Bali and Java; cassava grows wild on Mount Merapi's slopes in Java, and tea plantations dominate the landscape in western Java; papaya trees grow freely on Sumatra; and the tropical fish caught in the crystal-clear waters off Lombok are many and varied. The less fertile highlands of West Irian Jaya, however, produce only small quantities of sweet potato, while hilly Nusa Tengarra supports little more than corn.

For the best Indonesian food, visit Java, which is home to a wide variety of agricultural produce and many inspired, tasty dishes. In Javan cuisine, a simple plate of rice can be transformed into a feast that smells and tastes delicious. Spices such as turmeric and saffron tell the story of Indonesia's past, and the fiery chilli, which appears on every plate, reflects the warmth of the people.

*Left: The islands of Indonesia spread across the base of South-east Asia. The four main islands are Borneo, Java, Sumatra and Sulawesi.*

*Right: Indonesia is one of the world's largest producers of rice. Farmer's often use water buffaloes to help plough and prepare the rice fields for planting.*

## HOW TO USE THIS BOOK

Perhaps you have visited Indonesia and long to relive the tastes and scents of the food you ate there, or have enjoyed an Indonesian meal in a restaurant. Alternatively, you may enjoy Filipino, Indian or Malaysian food and want to discover related cuisines. Whatever the case, you will find plenty of information here about Indonesia's history, people and food. The introductory pages of this book will allow you to become familiar with the islands of Indonesia – not only with their geography but with their customs, feasts and festivals and, of course, their kitchens. There is an extensive guide, which introduces key ingredients from throughout Indonesia, and explains all the essential cooking techniques and practices you need to make authentic dishes.

Despite their complex flavours, the majority of cooks can prepare most dishes. There is not usually a need for specialist equipment, as most dishes are derived from traditional domestic recipes. Also, no two cooks ever interpret a recipe in exactly the same way, and ethnic cuisines have evolved over a long period of time and are never an exact science. Every cook or chef, new or established, has free licence to adapt a dish to suit the tastes of their family, community or customer and create wonderful meals from these exotic ingredients.

This superb collection of more than 80 dishes demonstrates how to make an array of mouthwatering dishes that are perfect for all occasions. Indonesian food is a wonderful explosion of tastes and colours. Use the best ingredients that nature offers and enjoy the tasty results.

*Far right: An Indonesian rice worker carrying the rice harvest.*

*Right: Sticky coconut crêpes are a popular street snack in Indonesia.*

Due in part to their location, the fertile green islands that comprise modern Indonesia have frequently been invaded. They have also traded with nations such as Malaysia, China, India, Persia, Arabia and Spain, as well as some European sea-going nations during the Spice Wars in the 16th and 17th centuries. This regular and long-term contact with foreign countries has had a significant impact on all aspects of Indonesian life, from religious beliefs and agricultural methods to culinary ingredients and cooking techniques – which are all still very much in evidence today.

### EARLY ANCESTRY

Archaeological research reveals the indigenous inhabitants to have been hunter-gatherers who subsisted on a diet of fruit, fish, taro and game. From c.4000BCE, repeated migrations from South-east Asia replaced them with a new Indonesian race that was mostly composed of Malays and sea-going Melanesians. It was not until the Dongson civilization spread from Vietnam and southern China around 3,000 years ago, however, that large cultural changes took place. The appearance of the Dongson initiated the spread of rice cultivation and irrigation across the islands, as well as the introduction of the water buffalo as both a beast of burden

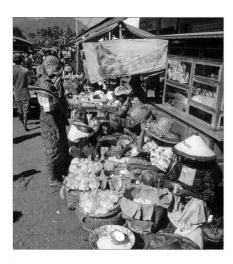

*Above: A typical street market in Bima, with local produce displayed in baskets lined with banana leaves.*

*Above: Lake Bralan, Bali, where the Pura Ulu Danau temple lies at the heart of a lush, flower-filled valley.*

and a source of food. The custom of sacrificing a buffalo was also adopted from the Dongsons and is still followed in Sumatra, Sulawesi and Nusa Tenggara.

By the 7th century BCE, the Indonesian archipelago was home to well-organized societies in which people tended irrigated rice paddies and raised domesticated water buffalo, chickens, pigs and dogs, and rural kitchens were stocked with foods such as bananas, breadfruit, coconuts and yams.

### TRADE INFLUENCES

In their early years, the islands that now form modern Indonesia were heavily influenced by the ingredients and cooking methods of China, India, Persia, Arabia and Malaysia. The Chinese traders and immigrants who visited the islands from the 7th century onwards brought ingredients such as noodles, rice and soy sauce, as well as the technique of stir-frying, which has become an integral part of the cuisine throughout the islands. Although Chinese dialects are rarely spoken today, and the government ruled that all original Chinese names had to be converted into Indonesian, there are still reminders of early Sino-Indonesian union in dishes such as lumpia and bak

mie goreng. They can easily be linked with the Chinese dishes of spring rolls and fried noodles, but have had indigenous herbs and spices added.

Chinese products and island spices, such as cloves and cinnamon bark, were traded for Indian, Persian and Arabian goods. The origin of the Indonesian curry, gulai or kare, can be traced back to these traders, since the spices in the dish (cardamom, cumin, coriander and garlic) all came from India. Trading links with these countries also introduced Hinduism and Buddhism to Indonesia, so bringing about a major change to the indigenous belief system. Islam was introduced in the 13th century, spreading from west to east, and was eventually adopted by most of the islands: the satellite kingdoms of the Majapahit were declared independent Muslim states. In spite of the ongoing presence of European sea-going nations during the Spice Wars in the 16th and 17th centuries (see below), Islam remained the dominant religion, spreading to most areas of the island chain. The result today is a Muslim population so large that it claims to be the biggest in the world.

The Spanish explorers of the 16th and 17th centuries brought with them unusual ingredients from the New World, such as corn, pineapples and tomatoes, as well as the

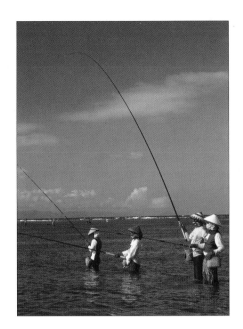

ubiquitous chilli pepper, which quickly became an essential part of many Indonesian dishes.

## THE SPICE WARS

Water was of vital importance to life in Indonesia. Oceans, rivers, streams and fertile deltas have affected the lives of the inhabitants as well as the way in which their cuisines have evolved. In fact, produce from waterways formed much of the early Indonesian diet. Water also brought traders and new culinary ideas, in addition to unusual goods from the Middle East and China.

Before the 16th century, Arab sailors who had visited the 'spice islands' of the East Indies (now known as Indonesia) sold spices to merchants at Constantinople, who then took them to Venice, where they were sold on to European merchants, who in turn took them to their own countries – a long and expensive chain. However, as the price of spices rose, these distant islands became ever more desirable to European traders who wanted to make money.

The first to arrive were the Portuguese in 1511. They captured the Malay port of Melaka and made large sums of money by trading there in cloves and

*Right: For families in Bali, social and religious gatherings tend to involve gifts of food and flowers.*

*Left: People fishing off Samur beach in Bali, wearing hats and masks to protect themselves from the sun's glare.*

nutmeg. The Spice Wars began when the Dutch reached the East Indies in 1596. By 1607 they had defeated the Portuguese and won control of the clove trade from Maluku as well as occupying the Banda Islands for their nutmeg. The English were drawn into the Spice Wars in 1601, setting sail under the auspices of the East India Company.

## EUROPEAN INFLUENCES

The European sea-going nations who were involved in the Spice Wars had limited influence on the culinary scene of Indonesia (although the introduction of tea was a major contribution).

Interestingly, nasi goreng, the egg-topped national fried rice dish, is one of the few dishes to trace its origins to a European country – Holland. Another Dutch influence is rijsttafel (rice table), which came from the village custom of holding a harvest-end feast, but has since evolved into an array of 12–30 side dishes served with rice – often with the misleading claim that it is an example of classic Indonesian cuisine. Indonesia was under Dutch dominance for some time, which accounts for Dutch influence in the cuisines, but the ethnic origins of many dishes remain strongly evident.

The cuisines of other Asian countries have more natural links with Indonesian cooking than those of Dutch and other European countries, but the colonial influences are still important and have added their own part to the story. One can conclude that the cuisine of Indonesia is largely shaped by history and enriched by the country's location.

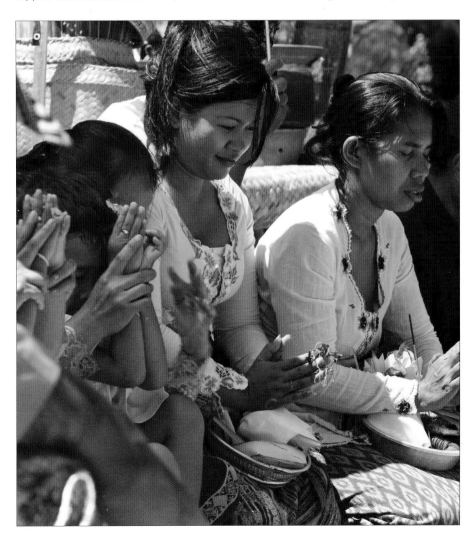

# INDONESIAN MEALS AND CUSTOMS

The home cooking of Indonesia is a relaxed affair, and the dishes all share a simplicity at their core. The attitude towards ingredients and preparation is matter-of-fact and open-minded: there are no strict rules, no correct or incorrect ingredients, just an acceptance that most dishes begin with a chilli-laced spice paste. Street food is popular in the cities, and most Indonesians enjoy a snack on the move during the day. This comes as no surprise when you see the amazing range of tempting snacks on offer at stalls and from roving vendors on every street.

### BREAKFAST

Indonesians start each morning with breakfast at sunrise, before the day starts to heat up. In the morning you can often see groups of women sitting outside their homes, chatting over bowls of rice topped with chillies and fried shallots. What Indonesians eat varies from region to region. In Java it might be just a bowl of rice left over from the day before, while in Maluku it could be a sago cake served with a cup of tea, and in Surabaya it might be a more substantial rice porridge with chicken. In rural communities, this first meal of the day is informal and snacks are eaten as minor sustenance as dawn breaks.

For a wealthy person in one of the large cities, however, a Western-style breakfast of a bowl of cereal and a cup of coffee is likely to be on the menu, although increasingly for Indonesians, breakfast tends to be a meal on the run, especially among urbanites.

### LUNCH AND SUPPER

It is traditional in many households to cook a large pot of rice in the morning, along with three or four dishes, which often include fish or meat, vegetables and a sambal, to go with it. The rice is often par-boiled and drained, then left in the pot to steam until it is fluffy and fully cooked. Doing this means that the cook can keep the rice warm for long periods of time while the other dishes, which are spread out on the table, are left all day for people to help themselves for lunch and supper. Both meals consist solely of what is on the table, which can be eaten in any combination or order as desired. In this type of meal, the rice (or any other staple) forms the main part of the meal, and diners spoon small helpings of the other dishes over it simply to flavour and moisten the grains. By contrast, more wealthy families may regularly eat thick curries, fried or grilled (broiled) meat and hearty fish or chicken dishes.

### STREET FOOD

All over Indonesia you can find *warungs* (casual, usually outdoor, food vendors, many operating in simple lean-to stalls) selling everything from cigarettes to rice and curries. These sellers play a very important role that is far more than just selling snack food: they are the pulse of social life; places where friends can meet and chat over some noodles or rujak; and a convivial stop on the way home on market day. Eating throughout Indonesia is a completely relaxed and informal experience, which means that *warungs* offer a home-from-home experience, but without the cooking or washing up! They epitomize the whole tradition of eating out, which is such a part of life in Indonesia that it is woven into the very fabric of the food culture.

*Above: There are several varieties of rice, and they can all be cooked and flavoured in many delicious ways.*

*Left: Indonesian meals usually include rice and lots of other small dishes.*

Most city-dwellers will eat at least one meal a day from a street seller, though for different reasons. For business people, the reason is that they are often simply too busy to cook, while country folk who have moved to the city often live in very basic accommodation with no kitchen, so they cannot cook for themselves. Luckily for both, there is a wide variety of snacks available all day long from the *warungs* and *kaki-limas* (roving vendors: literally 'five feet' – three for the cart and two for the vendor). The *kaki-limas* often specialize in just one type of snack, such as nasi goreng, or pisang goreng, which are sweet, sticky, deep-fried bananas.

## ETIQUETTE AND HOSPITALITY

If you are visiting an Indonesian home, your host will treat you with great respect, but you may find certain practices disconcerting at first. For instance, you may be invited to eat alone while your hosts sit and watch you. This is seen as a gesture of hospitality, showing that you are the priority, but it can be unnerving. Accept whatever food is offered with gratitude, but do not eat so much that there is not much left for the family. On large social occasions, wait until the host has motioned to you that you can start. The eldest member of a family will usually serve him- or herself first, but a guest may be allowed to jump the queue.

Indonesians usually like to eat with their hands, so the tradition of chopping ingredients into bitesize pieces before cooking them is highly practical. Use only your right hand to scoop up rice and other ingredients, and also use this hand for passing dishes around the table. (The left hand is strictly reserved for another bodily function, so to use it at the table would be a tremendous *faux pas*.) If you are left-handed, you will need to learn how to use your right hand for eating very quickly if you are to avoid causing offence. If hands are not appropriate, such as for a meal with a sauce, you will be given a fork and spoon to make eating easier. When you have finished, compliment the cook, then clean your teeth with a toothpick while covering your mouth with one hand.

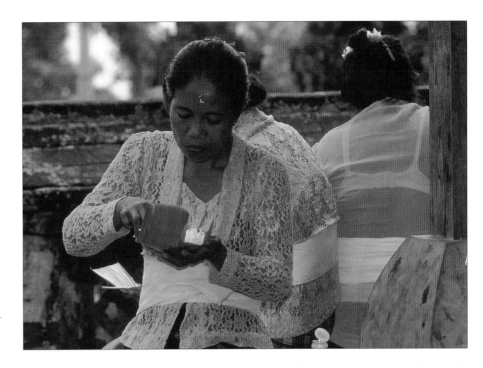

*Above: It is customary for Indonesians to eat with the right hand rather than with Western-style utensils.*

*Below: A colourful street market in Bali, with women carrying baskets of produce on their heads.*

# INDONESIAN FEASTS AND FESTIVALS

In Indonesia, Islamic holy events, such as Ramadan or Eid al-Adha, are marked either by fasting or by eating traditional foods, such as goat. By contrast, the Hindu communities traditionally prepare large feasts to celebrate family births, marriages and deaths, as well as making elaborate food offerings to present to their deities.

## RELIGIOUS OFFERINGS

Islam, Hinduism, Buddhism and Animism (the belief that everything has a soul, even inanimate objects such as rocks and vegetables) are practised with great enthusiasm, and the hunger of souls takes precedence over the hunger of the people. Festivals in other religions involve preparing food for the people to eat, but Indonesian special dishes are instead treated as reverent offerings to their different gods.

Rice lies at the essential heart of Indonesian life. Not only is it the staple food, which is central to every family meal, with the numerous dishes served alongside being mere accompaniments, but it is also held in high regard as the offspring of the goddess Dewi Sri. At the end of the fasting month that marks Ramadan, there is an hour of sunset prayer, known as *magrib*, when people come together to eat. Large amounts of sweetened tea are drunk with impressive quantities of food. This is a time when the food is for the believers, and not just for the gods.

The appeasement of the deities is of great importance to Hindu culture, most particularly in Bali, where their culinary needs are paramount. For instance, Galungan is a time when the souls of ancestors are said to come back to Earth to spend time with their families. Outside every home *penjors* (very tall, curved bamboo poles, each one decorated with banana and coconut leaves as well as fruit and flowers, rice and other tidbits) are erected in honour of the god of the mountain – Hyang Giri Pati. Offerings are also placed in shrines at the foot of the *penjors*. With spirits fêted and bodies and souls fed, harmony is believed to be maintained throughout the land.

*Above: Families in Seminyak, Bali, often gather on the beach to celebrate a variety of occasions, from births to religious festivals.*

## SELAMATANS AND OTHER FEASTS

Throughout its history, many religions have influenced Indonesia, and ritual celebrations are common affairs. Food is such an integral part of these festivities that there is even a name reserved for a meal prepared for a lot of people: *selamatan*. Such a meal is usually held at home to mark a family occasion, such as the birth of a child, a birthday, moving to a new house, the harvest, circumcisions and deaths. *Selamatans* will include a combination of meat, chicken and egg dishes, which are placed around the *tumpeng* – a

pyramid of yellow rice, the tip of which is offered to the eldest guest.

Meat is always served at celebratory feasts, especially cooked in traditional dishes such as rendang (slow-cooked buffalo or beef in coconut milk). While 90 per cent of the population of Indonesia is Muslim, and so does not eat pork, the Hindu island of Bali is an exception, and here feasts may revolve around a spit-roast pig.

Family weddings can range from a small domestic affair to a large feast, depending on the wealth of a family. A feast may last for several days and consists of a large buffet-style spread, which usually includes a spit-roast pig or goat. In Java, the bride feeds the groom by hand to symbolize her new role in life. Here there is also a feast for the seventh month of pregnancy, which involves seven dishes and seven hard-boiled eggs, which are skewered and placed in the main rice dish. If the feast is elaborate and beautifully presented, it is thought to predict the birth of a girl, whereas a less extensive collection of dishes will indicate a boy.

*Left: A young Hindu boy in traditional dress for Kuningan at the end of the Galungan Festival.*

## MUSLIM FESTIVALS

For most Indonesians, the main celebrations are Ramadan, the Muslim month of fasting, which ends with Eid al-Fitr, and Eid al-Adha (or Idul Adha) the Day of Sacrifice.

During the month of Ramadan, the devout must not eat or drink anything in the hours between sunrise and sunset, and many street vendors and other eateries shut for this period as a mark of respect. Once the sun has set, however, drums beat to call the faithful to prayer, and heaps of rice, along with meat and vegetable dishes, are brought out and eaten in company.

The end of the month of fasting is called Lebaran or Eid al-Fitr, and this is an occasion when many Indonesians go to see their families to ask forgiveness for any errors, and to drink sweetened black tea and sticky rice cakes. Ketupat (small coconut-leaf packets of steamed rice) are hung up as decoration and goodwill symbols.

Another important date on the Muslim calendar is Eid al-Adha, which commemorates Ibrahim's willingness to sacrifice his son Ishmael. Because God spared Ishmael, substituting a sheep in his place, it is traditional in Muslim cultures all over the world to sacrifice a sheep or goat to mark the event, and the meat is then shared among the family or wider community to be cooked in various ways. Eid al-Adha occurs 70 days after Eid al-Fitr; the animals that are marked for sacrifice are much in evidence as they are taken live to the market in the family car, in the backs of pick-up trucks or strapped on to the backs of bikes.

The Sekaten fair commemorates the prophet Mohammed's birthday, and huge cones of rice blended with many other ingredients, known as Gunangan Nasi, are taken to Kasunanan Palace in Surakarta. These are then blessed and distributed among the visitors around the Grand Mosque, to give prosperity and happiness in the coming year.

*Right: A procession of Hindu women in Bali carry carefully stacked and very elaborate food offerings for the gods.*

## HINDU FESTIVALS

Bali is particularly famous for its celebrations, when spicy regional dishes are cooked for the lively and colourful events on the Hindu calendar. These festivities include Kedaso, the festival of the tenth full-moon, and Penampahan, a festival of purification, when the gods are appeased with sacrificial pigs.

Wherever a deity may live, there you will find offerings of fresh fruit and food cooked specially for the gods. These offerings are frequently beautifully presented and can include impressive towers of fruit, small amounts of rice prettily held in banana-leaf pouches, and rice cakes made in fancy shapes. Whether you come across offerings in a rice paddy, a bus station or just a doorway, you must step around them carefully and move on, leaving them untouched. Daily offerings of rice, flowers and incense to the deities are also scattered along the edges of rice paddies to keep any demons away, and there is often a shrine to Dewi Sri, the Hindu goddess of rice and harvest, who is presented with fresh fruit and flowers.

Other food offerings, which may include home-grown vegetables and chickens, are made to mark the anniversary of the founding of a local temple. The people spend much of the day making rice cakes and decorations and preparing fruits, which they then assemble into stacks up to 1.8m/6ft high. Later, immaculately dressed women proceed to the temple with the beautiful foods carefully balanced on their heads. When the gods have eaten their fill, the leftovers are given to the community. At such celebrations, the gender roles are clearly defined: the men do the cooking and the women prepare the spices.

Other celebrations include Pager Wesi, where Hindus celebrate Sang Yang as the creator of the universe with offerings of food. At the Kasada festival, Javanese farmers of the fertile lands around Mount Bromo volcano process and throw food offerings, from fruit to livestock, into the crater for the deity.

# EQUIPMENT, TECHNIQUES AND INGREDIENTS

*The dishes of Indonesia tend to comprise of vegetables, meat*

*and fish, and using the freshest ingredients possible is*

*essential. This chapter looks at key equipment and foods,*

*ranging from rice and noodles to fruit and spices. The*

*following pages introduce the most common ingredients, and*

*discuss preparation and cooking techniques.*

# ESSENTIAL FLAVOURS

In Indonesian cuisine, it is vital that ingredients blend harmoniously on the plate, yet retain their flavours. The presence of five principal flavour notes – salty, bitter, sour, spicy and sweet – plays an important role in every Indonesian meal.

## CLASSIC INDONESIAN INGREDIENTS

The Indonesian kitchen boasts many fragrant spices that are gradually becoming more available to westerners: galangal, lemon grass, turmeric, kaffir lime leaves, the twisted pandanus (screwpine), cinnamon bark, cumin and coriander seeds, and cloves (although in Indonesia these are more likely to be used in scented cigarettes than food).

In parts of Indonesia where there is a history of Arab and Indian traders, such as Sumatra, many different local spices are used, but generally it is the chilli that is all important. In fact, the Indonesians' love of chillies means that they appear throughout a meal: in the bumbu at the start, chewed between mouthfuls during the meal, then in a sambal at the end. From their dominance of the cuisine, one would think that chillies are indigenous, but in fact they are a New World ingredient, which arrived in the 16th century.

Palm sugar (jaggery) is the primary sweetener, although cane sugar is sprinkled over fried bananas or in tea.

*Right: An Indonesian woman cooks in a rustic kitchen setting, Sumatra.*

The sour notes that are often detected in local recipes tend to emanate from tamarind, which is sold in dried or paste form in the markets, and is used liberally to cut through the oiliness of a dish.

Banana leaves are used for wrapping food that is going to be steamed or roasted, for wrapping soya beans and yeast together to make tempeh, or as a serving vessel or plate.

The flesh and water from freshly picked coconuts are free, and widely used in home kitchens, though coconut milk and other products can be bought. The oil from coconuts is often used for cooking, imparting a rich flavour.

## PASTES, SAMBALS AND SAUCES

Pungent pastes and fiery sambals are key aspects of Indonesian food. The first step of many dishes is to make a bumbu, which is a base paste made from crushed cumin, coriander seeds, cardamom, turmeric, shallots, garlic, ginger, lemon grass, cinnamon and chillies, which has coconut milk or stock added to it to make a paste.

Shrimp paste, terasi belacan, is made from small dried shrimp that are pummelled into a paste, then left for two weeks to dry out.

Sambals are particularly good for livening-up grilled (broiled) or deep-fried fish and for tempering the taste of roasted goat. The base ingredients are always chillies, garlic, shallots and salt: variations include shallots, sugar, tamarind, galangal and shrimp paste (sambal badjak), lime juice, lime rind, chillies, salt and vinegar (sambal jeruk) or chillies, lime and shrimp paste (sambal terasi).

Like sambals, dips and sauces are thought to be crucial to the whole enjoyment of a particular dish rather than an optional condiment. For example, bakmie goreng (Indonesian stir-fried noodles) and nasi goreng (Indonesian stir-fried rice) both rely on the ever-popular kecap manis, a thick, sweet soy sauce, for their essential flavour. When it comes to street food, these traditions adapt to modern tastes, and tomato ketchup appears in the Westernized stalls and bars.

## FINISHING TOUCHES

Garnishes are regarded as an important part of the meal. Crispy fried shallots, spring onions (scallions), sprigs of coriander (cilantro) and even fried eggs may be added to the dish at the end of cooking, but this does not mean that they are for decoration only: they are very much part of the dish and should not be left out.

*Left: Shrimp paste is fermented in the sun for two weeks.*

# SNACKS AND DRINKS

Along with most other culinary cultures of South-east Asia, the Indonesians prefer to eat fresh fruit at the end of a meal and sweet snacks during the day. This is because the meal is intended to be a balance of the five key flavours – salty, bitter, sour, spicy and sweet.

## SWEET FLAVOURS

In Indonesia, many of the traditional sweet snacks are made from glutinous rice, sweetened with sugar and flavoured with fragrant leaves, then steamed in tiny packages woven from palm fronds. The concept of ending a meal with something sweet is alien to the Indonesian culture, as sweet snacks are enjoyed at any time of the day.

Fresh fruit, on the other hand, is usually eaten at the end of the meal. With the abundance of tropical treats, the choice is always inspiring – watermelon, pomegranates, apples, pineapples, mangoes, jackfruit, mangosteens, snakeskin fruit, rambutan, sapodilla, passion fruit, sweet bananas and guava.

Generally, all these fruits are eaten fresh when ripe, but some are chosen when still immature to be chopped up for salads, such as rujak, a crunchy, fruity salad served with a spicy sauce.

*Below: Black sticky rice pudding (bubuh injin).*

## BEVERAGES

The Indonesians enjoy many fruit drinks but, as the nation is predominantly Muslim, home-made spirits and alcoholic beverages are consumed to a minimal degree. Among the many delectable and refreshing tropical fruit drinks and syrupy iced drinks is the delightfully refreshing es ketimun, made with shredded cucumber, sugar syrup and lots of ice.

*Below: Palm leaf flavours many sweet rice dishes.*

*Above: Fresh, spicy ginger tea (bandrek) is good for the digestion.*

In tea and coffee, Indonesia excels. Originally set up by the Dutch, the tea and coffee plantations are a feature of the stunning landscape tapestry of rice paddies. The majority of Indonesia's tea produce is of black tea, three-quarters of which is exported, but there is plenty left to satisfy the tea-drinking nation. Generally, tea is served black with sugar. Other teas include green tea and ginger tea, which is a popular morning beverage, particularly for peasants before they go to the fields.

Black tea is generally drunk among the Chinese communities and served in Chinese restaurants. A ginger-infused tea is drunk to aid the digestion, apart from in the hilly regions, where it is drunk at breakfast early in the morning.

Indonesia is also the third largest coffee producer in the world. Its coffee plantations are found in the highlands of Java and Bali and in Sulawesi and Sumatra. To drink coffee Indonesian-style, you need to think of it as a pick-me-up, rather than a pleasant after-dinner digestive. You can ask for milky coffee (kopi susu), which is served with sweetened condensed milk, or have black coffee (kopi tubruk), which is chewy, gritty and sweet.

# ESSENTIAL RECIPES

## BALINESE SPICE PASTE

The founding spirit of Balinese cooking, base gede can be used as a paste or a marinade in meat, poultry and fish dishes.

SERVES SIX TO EIGHT

INGREDIENTS
2 shallots, finely chopped
2 garlic cloves, finely chopped
25g/1oz fresh galangal, finely chopped
25g/1oz fresh turmeric, chopped
4 fresh red chillies, seeded and chopped
1 lemon grass stalk, chopped
5ml/1 tsp ground coriander
2.5ml/½ tsp ground black pepper
30ml/2 tbsp palm or vegetable oil
10ml/2 tsp terasi (Indonesian shrimp paste)
10ml/2 tsp palm sugar (jaggery)

**1** Using a mortar and pestle, grind the shallots, garlic, galangal, turmeric, chillies and lemon grass to a coarse paste. Beat in the coriander and black pepper.

**2** Heat the oil in a small, heavy-based pan, stir in the paste and fry until fragrant and just colouring. Stir in the terasi and sugar and fry for 2–3 minutes, until darker in colour. Remove from the heat and leave to cool. Store in a lidded jar in the refrigerator for up to 1 week.

**Per Portion** Energy 158kcal/654kJ; Protein 6.6g; Carbohydrate 8.9g, of which sugars 7.5g; Fat 13.6g, of which saturates 1.3g; Cholesterol 25mg; Calcium 126mg; Fibre 0.8g; Sodium 355mg.

## SHALLOT AND LEMON GRASS SAMBAL

In Indonesian kitchens, sambal matah is a master blend with multifarious uses as a marinade, curry paste and topping.

SERVES FOUR TO SIX

INGREDIENTS
2.5ml/½ tsp black peppercorns
10g/¼oz terasi
20 shallots, thinly sliced
5 garlic cloves, sliced
6 lime leaves, shredded
10 fresh red chillies, thinly sliced
4 lemon grass stalks, 2cm/¾in of root end very finely sliced
1 tsp salt
45ml/3 tbsp lime juice
1 tsp sugar
75ml/5 tbsp vegetable oil

**1** Crush the peppercorns using a mortar and pestle until grainy.

**2** Toast the terasi briefly over a live flame.

**3** Combine all the ingredients except the oil in a mixing bowl and blend well. Heat the oil and fry the sambal over a low heat for 8–10 minutes until the oil seeps out again.

**Per Portion** Energy 126kcal/520kJ; Protein 2.9g; Carbohydrate 7.5g, of which sugars 5.6g; Fat 9.6g, of which saturates 1.1g; Cholesterol 8mg; Calcium 51mg; Fibre 1.2g; Sodium 405mg.

## CHILLI AND SHRIMP PASTE

There is a saying in Indonesia: 'If your eyes do not water, the food is not good', which gives an indication of this highly popular paste's fieriness. This, like many other Indonesian pastes and spice blends, should be approached cautiously at first, but is bound to become a favourite condiment.

SERVES FOUR

INGREDIENTS

15ml/1 tbsp palm, groundnut (peanut) or vegetable oil
2 shallots, finely chopped
3 garlic cloves, finely chopped
4 spring onions (scallions), finely chopped
8 fresh red Thai chillies, seeded and finely chopped
10–15ml/2–3 tsp terasi (Indonesian shrimp paste)

**1** Heat the oil in a small wok or heavy-based pan. Stir in the shallots, garlic, spring onions and chillies and fry until fragrant and beginning to colour.

**2** Add the terasi and continue to fry for about 5 minutes, until dark and blended. Remove from the heat and leave to cool.

**3** Spoon the spice paste into a jar, cover and store in the refrigerator for up to 1 week.

**Per Portion** Energy 46kcal/191kJ; Protein 2.6g; Carbohydrate 2.2g, of which sugars 1.3g; Fat 3g, of which saturates 0.4g; Cholesterol 13mg; Calcium 44mg; Fibre 0.5g; Sodium 111mg.

## TAMARIND AND LIME SAUCE

This popular hot and sour dipping sauce is usually prepared for eating with freshly grilled fish or steamed shellfish. If you cannot find kalamansi limes for this or any recipes in this book, simply use the best limes you can buy – they should be glossy and plump with a zesty scent.

SERVES FOUR TO SIX

INGREDIENTS

juice of 2 kalamansi limes
30ml/2 tbsp tamarind paste
2 spring onions (scallions), white parts only, finely chopped
2 fresh red chillies, seeded and finely chopped

**1** Put the lime juice in a small bowl. Add the tamarind paste and mix together. Add a little water to thin the mixture until it is of dipping consistency.

**2** Stir in the spring onions and chillies. Spoon the sauce into a jar, cover and store in the refrigerator for up to 1 week.

**Per Portion** Energy 6kcal/23kJ; Protein 0.6g; Carbohydrate 0.6g, of which sugars 0.6g; Fat 0.1g, of which saturates 0g; Cholesterol 0mg; Calcium 10mg; Fibre 0.2g; Sodium 6mg.

## INDONESIAN PEANUT SAUCE

Also known as bumbu sate, this is a very popular dipping sauce for fried and grilled meats and steamed vegetables.

SERVES FOUR

INGREDIENTS
   30ml/2 tbsp groundnut
      (peanut) or vegetable oil
   1 shallot, finely chopped
   2 garlic cloves,
      finely chopped
   150g/5oz/¾ cup plus
      2 tbsp unsalted peanuts,
      finely ground
   15ml/1 tbsp terasi

   (Indonesian shrimp paste)
   15ml/1 tbsp palm
      sugar (jaggery)
   15ml/1 tbsp tamarind
      paste
   15ml/1 tbsp kecap manis
      (Indonesian sweet
      soy sauce)
   5ml/1 tsp chilli powder
   300ml/½ pint/1¼ cups
      water

**1** Heat the oil in a heavy-based pan, stir in the shallot and garlic and fry until golden brown. Add the ground peanuts, terasi and sugar and continue to fry for 3–4 minutes, until the peanuts begin to colour and release some of their oil.

**2** Stir in the remaining ingredients, bring to the boil, then simmer for 15–20 minutes until the sauce has reduced and thickened. Remove the pan from the heat and leave the mixture to cool, then blend in a processor to form a smooth sauce. Spoon into a jar, cover and store in the refrigerator for up to 1 week.

**Per Portion** Energy 309kcal/1284kJ; Protein 14g; Carbohydrate 10.9g, of which sugars 7.5g; Fat 23.6g, of which saturates 4.2g; Cholesterol 19mg; Calcium 77mg; Fibre 3g; Sodium 431mg.

## FRIED GRATED COCONUT

Indonesians rarely have a meal without this condiment on the side. Use freshly grated coconuts for a superior flavour. You should be able to buy coconuts readily from Asian supermarkets or your local grocer.

SERVES FOUR TO SIX

INGREDIENTS
   15ml/1 tbsp vegetable oil
   2 lemon grass stalks,
      2cm/¾in of root end
      very thinly sliced
   3 fresh red or green
      chillies, thinly sliced

   5 shallots, thinly sliced
   4 garlic cloves,
      thinly sliced
   175g/6oz freshly
      grated coconut
   5ml/1 tsp salt
   5ml/1 tsp sugar

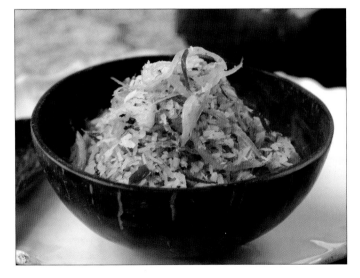

**1** Heat the oil in a wok and fry the lemon grass, chillies, shallots and garlic over a low heat for 2 minutes.

**2** Add the coconut and stir-fry for 10 minutes, tossing and turning constantly, until the coconut is light brown and the flavours are well incorporated.

**3** Add the salt and sugar and stir to blend thoroughly. Leave to cool and store in an airtight jar for up to 2 weeks.

**Per Portion** Energy 147kcal/606kJ; Protein 1.6g; Carbohydrate 3.2g, of which sugars 2.5g; Fat 14.3g, of which saturates 10.9g; Cholesterol 0mg; Calcium 9mg; Fibre 3g; Sodium 334mg.

## CUCUMBER AND PINEAPPLE RELISH

Acar is the generic term for pickles in Indonesia. Some will keep for a while, but this one must be eaten within a day or two.

SERVES FOUR

INGREDIENTS
1 cucumber, peeled, quartered lengthways and seeded
2.5ml/½ tsp salt
45ml/3 tbsp terasi (Indonesian shrimp paste)
6 fresh red chillies
45g/1½oz dried shrimps, soaked in hot water until soft
½ sweet pineapple, peeled, eyes and thick core removed
juice of 3 limes
5ml/1 tsp salt
5ml/1 tsp sugar

**1** Slice the cucumber flesh into diamond shapes, each 1cm/½in wide. Sprinkle with salt, toss well and set aside for 20 minutes.

**2** Toast the terasi over a live flame for 2 minutes until it is slightly charred and pungent, then grind with the chillies using a mortar and pestle until fine. Squeeze the moisture from the cucumber, handfuls at a time, into the mix. Set aside.

**3** Cut the pineapple into small chunks. Grind the dried shrimps until coarse with a mortar and pestle. Mix all the ingredients in a large bowl and adjust the seasoning to taste. Serve the relish as a side dish with coconut rice or curries.

**Per Portion** Energy 105kcal/446kJ; Protein 13.3g; Carbohydrate 11.9g, of which sugars 11.9g; Fat 0.8g, of which saturates 0.1g; Cholesterol 114mg; Calcium 298mg; Fibre 1.5g; Sodium 1715mg.

## SWEET AND SOUR SAUCE

Serve this sauce poured over fried poultry, or use it as a base for any sweet and sour recipe. It is a very familiar flavour to lovers of Chinese food, and really enlivens savoury rice-based meals if used as a condiment.

SERVES SIX TO EIGHT

INGREDIENTS
300ml/½ pint/1¼ cups water
30ml/2 tbsp sugar
45ml/3 tbsp tomato ketchup
15ml/1 tbsp lime juice
30ml/2 tbsp plum sauce
10ml/2 tsp cornflour (cornstarch)

**1** Combine all the ingredients except the cornflour in a small pan and bring the mixture to a slow boil.

**2** Blend the cornflour to a paste with a little water, add to the simmering mixture and cook, stirring well, until it is the consistency of pouring cream, adding more water if needed.

**3** Adjust with more water if it is too thick. Use as required, or store in the refrigerator until needed.

**Per Portion** Energy 284kcal/1209kJ; Protein 1.1g; Carbohydrate 74.1g, of which sugars 64.4g; Fat 0.1g, of which saturates 0g; Cholesterol 0mg; Calcium 27mg; Fibre 0.4g; Sodium 749mg.

# EQUIPMENT AND UTENSILS

Once, Indonesian kitchens were smoky sanctums with the aura of pungent wood smoke and strange cooking implements. The term 'dirty kitchen' applied to these old-fashioned cooking quarters, an area usually separate from the house. Contemporary lifestyles may dictate the need for high-tech appliances, but a few tools used in both countries are richly evocative of the agrarian way of life.

## CLEAVER

This heavy-bladed knife has more uses than it is given credit for. Originating in China and traditionally fashioned from iron – tempered steel is the modern norm – it has the weight and leverage that slices through solid bone. It slices, crushes and scoops in one fell swoop. Its blunt edge acts as a tenderizing tool much like a meat mallet. The ideal type is a single piece of tempered stainless steel, weighing in at 500g/1lb and measuring 30cm/1ft from the end of the handle to the blade tip. One or two small paring knives are all you need by way of additional cutting tools.

## COCONUT GRATER

There is nothing quite like grating your own shreds from fresh coconuts. Many specialist stores sell a version made of a wood-mounted sheet of heavy aluminium or brass and one fashioned from a whole piece of thick bamboo. They also come shaped from one piece of aluminium, with four legs.

*Above: The traditional coconut grater is a robust wood and brass structure.*

## MORTAR AND PESTLE

Fundamental to the process of grinding and pounding is the familiar mortar and pestle (it is called *lesong* in Indonesia), which came originally from India,

transplanted to most of South-east Asia. The pestle grinds dry spices, nuts and other hard ingredients to a cream. When you buy a new mortar, make sure it has high sides so that ingredients do not jump out.

## WOK

An implement that is the result of thousands of years of evolution, a wok or *kwali* or *kawali* serves for frying, braising, steaming and boiling. Cast iron ones, when seasoned with oil and cleaned, are best. Non-stick woks only last about a year before the special coating wears out. Stainless steel and aluminium woks conduct heat too rapidly.

When a trivet is placed in a wok and a lid is used, it becomes a steamer. Wok tools such as strainers for deep-frying, lids and long chopsticks often come as a set. Woks come with either one or two handles, the former being used more by chefs for tossing stir-fried dishes.

## WOK BRUSHES

An original Chinese design that has not changed for centuries, these are simply little makeshift brushes made from a bound cluster of fine strips of bamboo or rattan for cleaning out woks.

## TERRACOTTA POTS

Known as *belangah* in Indonesian, these are very much in use as they are ideal utensils for cooking anything with vinegar, as is typical of many Indonesian dishes.

## CLAY OR SAND POTS

Traditional Chinese clay pots have one handle. Those with a wire mesh frame are not meant for cooking on direct heat; they are gently heated and dishes cooked conventionally are transferred to them to be served at table. Originally meant for herbal and medicinal brews, they are now common everyday utensils for stews and braised dishes.

## SCOOPS AND LADLES

In metal, porcelain or coconut shell, these are useful for many specific purposes. Coconut shell ladles look

*Above: Bamboo is fashioned into many kitchen items. This is an unusually-shaped steamer basket for cooking rice.*

rustic and are pleasant to use. Some believe that they impart a special flavour to food, especially curries. It is more common today, however, for cooks to use stainless steel ladles, which are durable and easy to keep clean.

## WOVEN BASKETS

Bamboo is an extremely versatile material shaped into myriad forms and sizes for steaming, serving, ladling and storing. Rural folk are adept at fashioning palm and other pliant natural leaves into trays and baskets for winnowing and drying – for example, coconut palm fronds are rigid enough to be fashioned into plates and bowls, and their spines become skewers for satay. In Indonesia, woven bamboo baskets containing rice are placed above metal pots to act as steamers.

*Above: Brushes for cleaning woks are traditionally made from bundles of bamboo or rattan.*

### STEAMERS

Traditional Chinese bamboo steamers, dating back centuries, come in many sizes. As the material is porous, steam can escape and prevent condensation that can turn dishes mushy. They are totally organic and require only simple rinsing to clean. Modern variations include electric and microwave versions.

### BANANA LEAVES

Regarded as wrappers and throwaway plates, banana leaves are organic and more aromatic than foil. When made pliable after being blanched, they wrap all manner of foods for grilling (broiling), baking and steaming while imparting their distinctive perfume.

### LOTUS LEAVES

Of Chinese origin, dried lotus leaves have become popular as alternatives to banana leaves for steaming, but they are too delicate for direct heat. Fresh lotus leaves are not easy to obtain, but impart a lovely perfume to food.

### COOKIE CUTTERS

In Indonesia, small brass cookie cutters come in different shapes: stylized flowers, paisley and abstract designs. They are particularly useful for punching out shapes for identical, perfect batches of rice cookies.

### TWEEZERS AND CRIMPERS

Made of brass or iron, these little tweezers crimp and pinch designs on small cakes and cookies. Some come with tweezers at one end and a serrated roller at the other for making designs like leaves and other floral patterns.

### WOODEN CAKE MOULDS

Small abstract or floral designs are carved from a block of wood for pressing in rice and flour mixtures that are then knocked out gently for baking. Others are simple devices with heart-shaped or round designs that are pressed on to tart and cookie dough.

*Above: Two wooden cake moulds, used to shape cookie dough before baking.*

### CAKE PRESSERS, CUTTERS AND SCOOPS

In hard aluminium and mounted on wood or with a metal handle, pressers are meant for pressing down yam and

*Above: A tweezer and crimper with a selection of cookie cutters.*

radish cakes or glutinous rice bases with sweet toppings for steaming. Cutters, either plain or serrated, are used for making linear or curvy cuts of rolled dough or other cooked, soft bakes and jellies. Small oval scoops are made extra thin for lifting soft and delicate silken tofu so that it doesn't break up.

### JELLY MOULDS

Mostly made from metal or plastic these days, jelly moulds are used for the very popular sweet jellies and agar agar items. Designs range from fish, pineapple and turtle shapes to traditional ridged ones. Being mainly small, they are easy to unmould with a gentle tap on the sides.

### NOODLE STRAINERS

Traditional noodle strainers are made of brass or aluminium wire mounted on a bamboo handle. They are used for straining and scooping noodles and vegetables out of hot oil or cooking liquid. This is a particularly useful item for deep-frying spring rolls and other popular snacks and appetizers.

*Left: A single-handled wok is good for stir-frying; a double-handled wok is better for steaming and deep-frying.*

*Above: A wire mesh noodle strainer is a traditional kitchen implement that is still regularly used in modern kitchens.*

# COOKING TECHNIQUES

The technique most employed by the Indonesian cook, as a preparation for the main cooking, is the grinding and then sautéing of spice pastes in a wok or small pot. There is a strict order of what goes in first: hard, dry herbs such as lemon grass, garlic and candlenuts are ground first, to provide a 'cushion' for wet ones such as onions and chillies, so that bits don't fly out of the mortar. The sautéing step imparts the intrinsic flavour to many dishes. The watchwords are 'when the oil separates', meaning the spices are adequately fried and ready for the next step.

Indonesian cooks fry their spices for the same reason – to extract the rich flavours in which to bathe meats, poultry and vegetables. Aromatics such as shallots, garlic and onions are used with abandon and then blended with fermented seafood sauces such as terasi for an intoxicating blend of tastes and aromas.

## STIR-FRYING

Used for the most basic and simplest of dishes, stir-frying is a method that has evolved over centuries in China, and is indispensable for a whole range of dishes that need to be cooked quickly.

In Indonesia, the pre-blanching of vegetables to preserve their colour and crispness is almost *de rigueur*, and results in exquisite textures. Intense heat and constant motion ensure that food cooks evenly in minutes. This is where the *kawali* or *kwali* (wok) reigns supreme.

*Above: Marinated, skewered chicken, ready for the barbecue.*

## MARINATING

When not initially fried, spice blends still impart flavour to many foods – from fruits to meat – as a tenderizing and fragrant marinade. The Indonesians tend to find simple boiled or roasted meat bland. Local meat like buffalo, goat and pork may not be of particularly good quality and thus needs to be tenderized with marinades.

*Left: Stir-frying is a quick and healthy method of cooking vegetables.*

*Below: Wrapping food in leaves before grilling helps flavours develop.*

*Above: Dim sum, breads and desserts are often steamed rather than baked.*

Vinegar has great affinity with soy sauce, sugar and other indigenous ingredients such as annatto seeds, kalamansi lime and black pepper. Once blended, the mixture is fried with vegetables, meat or seafood and this has a 'pickling' effect.

## STEAMING

The classic method of cooking rice in Indonesia is to steam it in a cone of woven bamboo, inserted over a metal or clay pot of boiling water, or a traditional bamboo steamer like those brought in by early Chinese migrants. However, rice is now more often cooked in an automatic rice cooker, which is widely considered a must-have in modern homes. Many other foods, including breads, fish and desserts, are gently cooked in a traditional bamboo steamer over a pan of water on the hob. This keeps food moist and locks in flavour.

## SLOW-COOKING AND BRAISING

With the unhurried pace of life in some areas, slow-cooking methods evolved as much for the need to soften tough meat fibres as for spices to be steeped. Simmering or braising is common to all kitchens and is usually done in a wok in Indonesia. This achieves results that are similar to casseroling, but the latter is cooked in an oven. It was traditional that the meal was ready on the workers' return from the fields.

*Above: Braising meat in a wok allows the rich flavours and spices to infuse.*

## GRILLING (BROILING) OR BARBECUING

The modern deep-fat fryer found in Western kitchens is rarely used, and grilling (broiling) is the universal method of cooking that comes closest to deep-frying. In Indonesia, any roasting is usually done by placing food in a covered clay pot set over a wood fire for long cooking. Charcoal grilling, on the other hand, is widely practised in homes, restaurants and by hawkers. Roasting and charcoal grilling are techniques employed in kitchens throughout Indonesia.

## WRAPPING

Throughout the islands, banana leaves are revered as the means to perfect flavours, and wrapping things in them is a craft as ancient as the land itself. The leaf is resilient, pliant and aromatic, so the food it wraps comes away with a distinct perfume that is hard to categorize. The wrapped ingredients may be cooked either by steaming or grilling. As a 'green' material, it has few peers for versatility, sustainability and sheer flavour, and there is an endless supply in the urban and rural areas.

*Below: Spiced fish wrapped in a banana leaf steams to perfumed perfection on a traditional bamboo rack, which is positioned over a water-filled wok.*

# RICE

This grain has been a staple crop throughout most of tropical Asia for many generations, and it is around a communal bowl of comfortingly hot, fluffy white rice that most meals are built. For good reason, rice is regarded as the 'staff of life' and some superstitions connected to its power still hold sway. Rice agriculture is bound up with reverent rites and near mystical rituals, in which offerings are made to the rice deity. In every rice-eating household, there is invariably a large barrel or tin in which the raw rice is stored. As the last few grains are reached families hurriedly top the container up to the brim for fear of attracting bad luck or negative energy.

The 'rice bowl' areas in Indonesia are concentrated in Java, Sumatra and Bali. These terraces are an architectural marvel, rising like stairways up almost vertical hillsides that can top several thousand metres in height.

No one knows for sure why these rice fields were built so high up and against such fatiguing odds. Perhaps the Ifugao, once farmers in the plains, may have been driven into the hills by invaders, but the remarkably unchanged terraces are still there and

*Below: Terraced rice paddies in Sumatra, Indonesia.*

*Right: Fragrant jasmine rice has tender, aromatic grains. It is widely available in supermarkets.*

still worked. They are truly a beautiful and almost mystical sight.

In times past, freshly harvested rice was pounded in an enormous pestle and mortar and then winnowed to remove the husk and bran before it could be cooked. Commercial milling of rice began in the mid-19th century and today, most processing is done mechanically except in family-owned smallholdings.

## RICE DISHES

There are only two methods of cooking rice for basic sustenance: boiling and steaming. But the precious grain is by no means confined to being boiled and eaten unadorned. Once cooked thus, it can be used as the basis of many other dishes. Indonesian cooking in particular has elevated rice to delicious heights, matched by few others for spicy ingenuity. Rice with fragrant spice pastes rich in lemon grass, garlic, chillies and ginger; rice tinted a glorious yellow with turmeric, enriched with groundnut (peanut) oil and coconut

milk, tossed with seafood, meats and vegetables – it is a glorious palette of flavours, colours and textures.

Given that rice comes in many different forms – long grain, short grain, sticky, jasmine (fragrant) – the preferences throughout Indonesia vary greatly from region to region, from village to village and even from family to family. In general, jasmine is preferred for everyday meals when eaten plain. Good quality jasmine rice has a subtly delicate scent, with dry, thin and firm grains that are translucent when raw. Boiled or steamed, the texture should be firm and still retain some bite. The colour should be a pristine white and when you rake it with a fork, it should fluff up nicely. Long grain rice tends to be reserved for more important occasions, ceremonial meals and ritual offerings, when spices such as saffron or turmeric are added to impart a golden colour and a delicate scent.

## LONG GRAIN RICE

There is some confusion with reference to the types of rice, but there is one simple explanation based on usage. Short grain or pudding rice is for desserts and long grain is for meals with savouries. Basmati, Patna (Indian long grain), Thai fragrant and sweet (Japanese or short grain) rice are not brand names but denote where they come from. They are in effect variety names.

Basmati has the longest grain of all in proportion to its grain size, and peculiarly becomes longer and not wider when cooked. Basmati rice, with its distinctive, nutty flavour, while indigenous to India and Pakistan, is also grown in Indonesia. The town of Cianjur in West Java is reputed to produce the best long grain.

## SHORT GRAIN RICE

When a meal calls for rice gruel, known as congee among the Indonesian Chinese, short grain rice is preferred. It is served with a wide range of pickles, stir-fries and simple dishes. The Indonesian name for this gruel is bubur.

## GLUTINOUS RICE

Sticky or glutinous rice can be either short or long grain and the glutinous reference is something of a misnomer. Rice contains no gluten at all; it is the high starch content that gives this rice its sticky, glutinous texture. Usually destined for sweet snacks and desserts as the starch compacts when cooked, glutinous rice is also popular in some regions to soak up spicy curry gravies and palm sugar (jaggery). All types of rice contain a certain amount of starch, and all are gluten-free.

In the more urban spots such as Jakarta, varieties imported from Thailand and Malaysia, whether long grain or jasmine, are eaten widely. These tend to contain relatively high levels of starch; hence the produce of these regions is known as 'sticky rice' or 'glutinous rice'. There are two kinds of starch in any cereal grain: amylase and amylopectin. Sticky rice is high in the latter, and when the rice is cooked, these molecules form a gel, enclosing water within their strands.

Glutinous rice comes in both long and short grain varieties. The grains have to be soaked for several hours, sometimes overnight, before cooking. For festive dishes such as saffron or turmeric rice for Indonesian rituals and weddings, it is turned out as savoury offerings, often perfumed with rose water, cinnamon and cloves. It is rarely boiled and eaten plain as part of a meal, unless for a special occasion such as the Dutch-inspired Rijstaffel in upmarket hotels in Indonesian cities. Fundamentally, glutinous rice mainly lends itself to the making of dumplings, puddings and festive sweets.

In contrast to normal long grain rice, the highly polished, glutinous rice grain is an opaque white colour when raw, and turns translucent when cooked. Although the texture of cooked glutinous rice is quite firm, it is nevertheless sticky and clumps together like a lump of dough. It is this doughy characteristic that makes it popular as a wraparound for a range of filled rice dishes. In Indonesia, lemper is a favourite snack of sticky rice filled with spicy meat or seafood.

## BLACK GLUTINOUS RICE

This unpolished, wholegrain glutinous rice is almost exclusively used for sweet dishes. When soaked in water and cooked, the grains turn a deep reddish-purple. In Indonesia this is called ketan hitam, and cooked with coconut milk and palm sugar. It must be soaked for several hours or overnight before cooking. Black sticky rice is available in some Asian markets.

## GROUND RICE OR RICE FLOUR

Used in making all kinds of sticky sweets and cakes, ground rice is also a thickener, used similarly to cornflour (cornstarch) or arrowroot. Rice flour is made by grinding the raw grain very finely. Long grain and medium grain rice flour is used to make dough for fresh and dried rice noodles, as well as for dumplings, crêpes and buns. Glutinous rice flour, sometimes called sweet rice flour, is reserved for sweet pastries, pancakes and cakes. Do not confuse this with rice powder, which is much finer and is used in delicate bakes. All types are available from Asian stores and should be kept in an airtight container.

## RICE PAPERS

Originally found only in Thai and Vietnamese cuisines, delicate triangular or circular rice papers and wrappers have been adopted by Indonesian chefs. Rice papers are now used widely as a skin for spring rolls. Made from rice flour, water and salt, they are brittle to hold and need to be soaked briefly in hot water until they are soft and pliable. Lift each wrapper out with a chopstick and spread it on a chopping board before topping with filling. Once rolled up, they can be eaten as they are or deep-fried. Dried rice papers are available in Asian stores and some supermarkets.

Spring rolls are usually deep-fried. Freshly cooked pork, prawns (shrimp), beansprouts and vermicelli are wrapped in rice paper, which has been dipped in cold water until it is pliable and transparent.

*Below: Black and white glutinous rice.*

### RICE WINE AND VINEGAR

Local rice wine is used less in the Muslim regions of Indonesia, where people nonetheless eat fermented rice in desserts called tapai, disregarding its alcoholic content.

### PREPARING AND COOKING RICE

Many people find difficulty in preparing soft, fluffy rice. There are actually few fundamental rules. Most rice grains are cooked using the absorption method, except glutinous rice, which is soaked and steamed. The timings and amounts of water given here relate to white rice. Brown rice needs a longer cooking time.

### Washing rice

Traditionalists will insist that rice goes through 'seven changes of water' but most of the rice bought in supermarkets today requires minimal washing to whirl away traces of husks or discoloured grains. However, long grain rice does benefit from rinsing in cold water to reduce the excess starch, so that the cooked grains separate easily.

**1** Put the rice into a bowl and cover with cold water. Swirl until the water becomes cloudy, then leave to settle.

**2** Drain the rice in a sieve (strainer) then return it to the bowl and repeat until the water is clear.

### Soaking

Some chefs soak rice before cooking. This is said to make the rice intensely white. Increasing the moisture content of the grains also means that the cooking water can penetrate more effectively, resulting in fluffier rice.

After rinsing the rice, leave the grains in the bowl and cover with cold water. Leave to soak for half an hour. Drain the rice through a sieve (strainer), rinse it under cold water, then drain again.

If you are using brown rice, soaking it for two hours in warm water prior to cooking activates the enzymes and optimizes its nutritional content.

### Cooking by absorption

Rice soaks up a lot of water as it cooks – 450g/1lb of uncooked rice will absorb up to 600ml/1 pint of water, making enough to feed four moderate appetites.

The proportion of water required and the cooking time will both vary slightly with different grains, so it is wise to follow the instructions on the packet if you are cooking an unusual variety. Put the measured grains and water into a heavy pan and cook the rice until all the water has been absorbed. The old method is to add enough water to come up to two joints of the index finger from the top of the rice.

### Boiling rice

This method is suitable for most types of rice, especially long grain.

**1** Prepare the rice and put it in a large pan. Pour in about 1.2 litres/2 pints/5 cups for every 200g/7oz/1 cup rice and add a pinch of salt. Bring back to the boil, then lower the heat and simmer, uncovered, for the time indicated on the packet, or until the rice is tender.

**2** Drain the cooked rice in a sieve or strainer and rinse thoroughly with plenty of hot water. Then return the rice to the pan or set the sieve over the pan.

**3** Cover with the pan lid or a dish towel and leave the rice to stand for about 5 minutes. Before serving, use a fork to fluff up the rice, adding a litte butter or oil if you like.

### Steaming rice

Rice that is to be steamed should be cooked in a covered, flat vessel such as a shallow pan or bamboo steamer with just enough water to cover it. Test if the rice is cooked by eating a few grains.

**1** Fill a wok one-third full with water. Place a bamboo steamer, with the lid on, over the wok and bring the water underneath to the boil.

**2** Lift the lid off the steamer and place a dampened piece of clean muslin (cheesecloth) over the rack. Put the rice in the middle and spread it out a little. Fold the edges of the muslin over the rice, put the lid back on the steamer and steam for about 25 minutes, until the rice is tender but still firm.

### Using an automatic rice cooker

Once the preserve of the Japanese, rice cookers are now one of the most popular and simplest ways of cooking rice. Simply wash and drain the rice, place it in the inner cooker bowl with the requisite amount of water, and switch the rice cooker on. When the rice is cooked, the steamer will automatically switch itself off. It works by weight, with the inner pot resting on a springboard. When all the water is absorbed, the rice cooker switches off automatically.

### Cooking in a microwave

Prepare the rice as for a rice cooker, but do not cover the pot as the water will boil over. For 250g/9oz rice you will need 300ml/½ pint water, though long grain rice may need a little more.

# NOODLES

Ubiquitous in Indonesia, noodles came by way of China several centuries ago and are now firmly within the mainstream of both schools of cooking. Noodles are consumed in great quantities as snacks and main meals. If the main dish doesn't contain rice it will consist of noodles. They are eaten at all hours of the day, in soup for breakfast, simply stir-fried for a filling snack, or incorporated into main dishes with meat, fish and vegetables.

It is no wonder that most food stalls in Indonesian villages and towns serve both staples in many combinations. The common name for noodles in Indonesia is mee or mie, as in mee (mie) goreng or spicy fried noodles. It also pops up in richly sauced dishes such as mee rebus (boiled noodles in spicy gravy), mee Siam (a derivative from Siam, the ancient name for Thailand), and mee soto (spicy soup noodles).

Noodle stalls are found throughout Indonesia and in the dozens of *warungs* or hawker centres; each includes many stalls selling the different types. A favourite in Indonesia is laksa, a rich, coconut milk-based noodle dish with lashings of chilli paste and laksa leaves.

Noodles are made from either rice or wheat flour, and the everyday ones fall into several main types. Mee are made from wheat flour, sometimes with egg, and are either thin and long or flat, much like tagliatelle pasta strands.

Wheat noodles come in a wide range of types, many from China, and are usually sold dried, in packets.

Rice noodles also come in a variety of shapes. Long, flat noodles are called rice sticks or kway teow in the Chinese Swatow dialect. There is a very thin noodle variously called translucent vermicelli or glass noodles, known as sohoon in Indonesian. This type of noodle, however, is made from mung bean flour.

## FRESH RICE NOODLES

Many daily markets and supermarkets in Indonesia sell rice noodles, supplied fresh by local manufacturers. They are sometimes frozen but are mainly sold chilled, in packets. Some wet markets in rural areas stock them loose in basins, and customers simply ask for them by weight.

## FINE RICE NOODLES

Commonly called rice vermicelli, there are several types of varying thicknesses, all sold in dry form. Most come from China or Thailand, but increasingly local manufacturers in Indonesia are producing instant noodles in self-contained snack pots.

## RICE STICKS

Though not in widespread use, dry rice sticks are useful because of their long shelf-life. They are gradually becoming

*Right: Dried vermicelli rice noodles should be soaked, not boiled.*

more popular among busy people who do not have time to buy the fresh variety daily. They are simply briefly boiled or blanched, depending on the type. Generally much thinner than the fresh variety, they are ideal for soups but tend to break up easily when fried.

## WHEAT FLOUR NOODLES

Generally pale yellow, these come either dried to be reconstituted or fresh to be blanched before use in stir-fries or curries. There are three distinct types: factory-produced dried skeins of yellow noodles that have to be boiled for a few minutes or longer depending on the type; freshly made and semi-dry noodles, usually with a light coating of flour, that need only to be blanched; and fresh yellow noodles that need very light cooking.

Some producers oil their fresh yellow noodles, and these must be blanched thoroughly to remove the grease. Dry noodles, like rice sticks and vermicelli, double in bulk when reconstituted but fresh ones remain the same.

Some wheat noodles contain egg and resemble Japanese udon. They are often referred to as Shanghai-style noodles, and are usually sold fresh. They are firmer and denser than rice noodles and are used in stir-fries and soups. Fairly new to the market is a more nutritious variety where the dough is blended with spinach, which colours the noodles pale green.

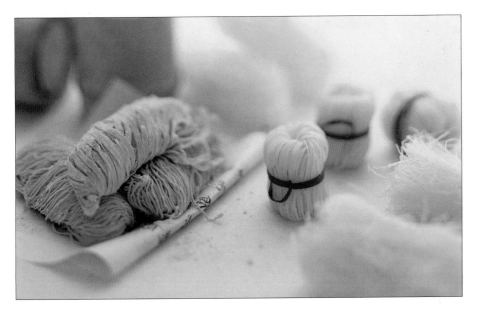

*Left: Noodles of various shapes and textures, made from rice, mung bean or wheat flour, are popular in broths and stir-fries.*

## MUNG BEAN NOODLES

Called by many names, including transparent noodles, translucent vermicelli, cellophane or glass noodles – these are made from mung bean flour and are always sold dry. They reconstitute rapidly when soaked in warm water and have the peculiar characteristic that they keep their crunch no matter how long you cook them. Usually sold in small skeins, they have a neutral flavour that soaks up seasoning very well, and are often simply cooked in stock.

## HAND-TOSSED NOODLES

A recent import from north China, hand-tossed noodles are made fresh in restaurants, more as a theatrical event than to meet consumer demand – something like hand-tossed pizza. It takes years of practice to be able to knead wheat flour into a firm but elastic dough, then pull and stretch it repeatedly until fine threads appear before your eyes. Most restaurants that offer this dish charge a premium price for it, as only a limited amount of these ultra-fresh noodles can be made each day.

### Preparing rice noodles

Fresh rice noodles need to be blanched briefly in hot water and drained before use in soups or stir-fries. Vermicelli, on the other hand, need only to be soaked for about 20 minutes.

Dried rice noodles double in bulk when rehydrated. Once prepared this way, they should not be cooked for too long or they turn mushy and break up. About 150g/5oz of reconstituted noodles are sufficient for one portion, as each bowl will also contain vegetables, meat or seafood.

## TO MAKE FRESH RICE NOODLES

A variety of dried noodles are available from Asian stores and supermarkets in the West, but fresh ones are quite different and if you do want to make them, it's not that difficult. For a snack, fresh noodle sheets can be covered in sugar or honey, or dipped into a sweet or savoury sauce of your choice. Alternatively, you can cut them into wide strips and gently stir-fry them with garlic, ginger, chillies and nuoc mam or soy sauce – a popular local snack.

As a guide, to serve four you will need about 225g/8oz/2 cups rice flour and 600ml/1pint/2½ cups water. You will also need a wide pot with a domed lid, or a wok lid, a piece of thin, smooth cotton cloth (such as an old clean sheet) and a lightly oiled baking tray.

### Preparing the batter

**1** Place the flour in a bowl and stir in a little water to form a smooth paste. Gradually pour in the rest of the water, whisking all the time to make sure there are no lumps. Beat in a pinch of salt and 15ml/1 tbsp vegetable oil. Set aside for 15 minutes.

**2** Meanwhile, fill a wide pot with water. Cut a piece of cloth a little larger than the top of the pot. Stretch it over the top of the pot (you may need someone to help you), pulling the edges down over the sides so that the cloth is as taut as a drum, then wind a piece of string around the edge, securing the cloth with a knot or bow.

**3** Using a sharp knife, make 3 small slits, about 2.5cm/1in from the edge of the cloth, at regular intervals. If you need to top up the water during cooking, pour it through these slits. Check that the cloth remains very taut.

### Cooking the noodle sheets

**1** Bring the water in the pot to the boil. Once it is bubbling and steam is rising through the cloth, stir the batter and ladle a portion (roughly 30–45ml/ 2–3 tbsp) on to the cloth, swirling it to form a 10–15cm/4–6in wide circle.

**2** Cover the pot with the domed lid and steam for 1 minute, until the noodle sheet is translucent. To remove it, carefully insert a spatula or round-bladed knife under the edge of the noodle sheet and gently prize it off the cloth – if it doesn't peel off easily, you may need to steam it for a little longer.

### COOK'S TIP

You may have to top up the water through the slits. The cloth might need to be tightened over the pot, otherwise the batter will form a pool in the centre.

**3** Transfer the sheet to the oiled tray and repeat with the rest of the batter. As they accumulate, stack the sheets on top of each other, brushing the tops with oil so they don't stick together. Cover the stack with a clean dish towel to keep them moist.

**4** Cut the noodle sheets into ribbons with a pasta machine or pizza cutter.

# VEGETABLES

Raw, stir-fried, braised, pickled or salted, vegetables are worked into every meal in some manner in Indonesia. Almost every meal includes a vegetable side dish or a spicy salad, pickled or as raw leaves to serve Ulam-style. It is intrinsic within both cuisines that a meal must be balanced with vegetables, protein and starch. Texture is also important, so 'salads' might include such ingredients as fruit, meat, shellfish and tofu.

## AUBERGINES (EGGPLANTS)

Technically fruits, although eaten as vegetables, aubergines (or brinjals as they are known in Indonesia) came originally from India and Thailand. The most common aubergine is long and thin, in shades of pale green and purple. This is the most popular variety, as the flavour is sweet with very little bitterness. Incredibly versatile, it is added to stews, curries and stir-fries, and the flesh absorbs all the delicious spices and flavours of the dish.

Aubergines are never eaten raw in Indonesia. When choosing, look for smooth, unblemished skin and firm flesh. There are also smaller varieties that range from green to purple and yellow, or are small and round, that are much loved by the Indonesians. These streaky pale green and cream-coloured aubergines are usually halved and added to curries. The tiny, green pea aubergines are also popular throughout South-east Asia. The size of garden

*Below: Aubergines (eggplants) come in different sizes and varieties of purple.*

*Above: Bamboo shoots need to be peeled and sliced before use.*

peas, these aubergines grow in clusters and have a slightly bitter taste with a pleasantly crunchy texture. They are available in Asian stores and some supermarkets.

The majority of aubergines found in stores and supermarkets are either glossy purple or almost black and can be long and slim or fat like zeppelins. All have a similar bland yet smokey flavour and the flesh is spongy to touch when raw, but soft after cooking.

## BAMBOO SHOOTS

Technically a giant grass, bamboo has many important uses. The long, thin stems or 'trunks' are used for making baskets, furniture and even as containers for rice to be roasted in and split open afterwards. Bamboo trunks are also artfully shaped and made into kitchen utensils, such as steamers, strainers and chopsticks. The leaves

*Above: If you cannot find long beans, use French or green beans instead.*

(usually dried) are used as wrappers for Chinese dumplings or steamed rice dishes, imparting their own unique flavour to the dish.

The small shoots that are dug up just before they emerge from the ground are very tasty. Fresh, pickled or dried, bamboo shoots are popular throughout Indonesia, and are a key ingredient in spring rolls and stir-fries. With older shoots, the outer sheath is stripped off and the tough base removed. Once peeled, the pale yellow inner core is sliced and boiled for at least half an hour before it is edible. The smaller, pale yellow or creamy-white, fresh young shoots need only be blanched briefly. They have a wonderful texture and flavour and are delicious added to stir-fries, curries and soups. Dried shoots, mainly from China, require long soaking before use. Fresh shoots are available in Asian stores, but cans of ready-cooked shoots preserved in brine can be bought in most stores.

## YARD-LONG BEANS

Sometimes referred to as 'snake beans' or 'chopstick beans', these long, green beans are the immature pods of black-eyed beans (peas) and can measure up to 60cm/2ft in length. Generally they are cooked in curries, boiled or stir-fried with sambal or chilli paste, garlic and ginger. Pencil-thin and dark or light green in colour, they are available fresh in Asian markets.

## GOURDS AND SQUASHES

Frequently used in Indonesian cooking, gourds and squashes are often stuffed and fried, steamed or boiled, and sliced for stir-fries and curries.

### Bitter melon

This gourd is considered nutritious and medicinal, as it contains high levels of quinine. Before cooking, the gourd needs to be slit lengthways to remove its red seeds and inner membrane. The outer shell is then sliced into half-moons and stir-fried, blanched or pickled or added to curries. If you want to remove some of the bitterness, sprinkle a little salt on the slices, leave for 10 minutes and then squeeze out the moisture.

Bitter melons are sold fresh in most Asian stores. A firm, green bitter melon should be allowed to ripen a little before use and will keep for 3–4 days, but a soft yellowish one should be used within a day or two.

### Luffa squash

Dark green with ridges running lengthways, luffa squash has sweet and spongy flesh and is usually harvested when it is about 30cm/1ft long. The outer skin is tough and inedible and has to be removed to reveal the soft, white flesh. Generally, it is sliced and used in stir-fries, omelettes and soups, much the same way as you would cook a courgette (zucchini). Luffa has a mild, delicate flavour very similar to that of cucumber. Luffa is mostly used in stir-fries or soups. It goes particularly well with mild-tasting foods such as chicken, fish and shellfish, which do not overwhelm its delicate flavour. Luffa

*Above: The bitter melon looks like a knobbly cucumber.*

*Right: Straw mushrooms are a popular ingredient.*

*Above: Young, fresh luffa can simply be washed and do not need to be peeled.*

squash is available in Asian markets. Unlike cucumber or young, tender courgettes, luffa is never eaten raw. Keep fresh luffa in the refrigerator, but do not store it for too long, as within 2–3 days of purchase it will start to go limp. Luffa are also known as Chinese okra, silk squash and sponge gourd.

## WINGED BEAN

This unusual vegetable is widely used as a salad vegetable and also stir-fried with spices in Indonesia. When not overcooked they have a desirable crunch. Cut into small pieces, they have an interesting four-winged shape with small edible seeds in the centre.

## MUSHROOMS

Available fresh, dried or canned, mushrooms are used in soups, stir-fries, stews, broths and braised dishes.

### Straw mushrooms

Also called bulb mushrooms, straw mushroom caps look like tiny brown eggs. The whole mushrooms are often used in braised dishes for visual appeal and texture. Once peeled, they reveal small dark-brown caps and stocky, cream-coloured stems which look lovely in clear broths. Very delicate in flavour and texture, straw mushrooms are available dried, fresh and in cans. Canned mushrooms must be drained and thoroughly rinsed before use.

### Oyster mushrooms

In the wild, oyster mushrooms grow in clumps on rotting wood. The caps, gills and stems are all the same colour, which can be pearl grey, pink or yellow.

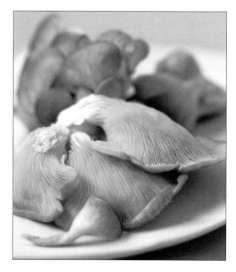

*Above: Oyster mushrooms have a wonderful flavour and texture.*

The flavour is mild, with a hint of seafood. Oyster mushrooms are popular in soups and stir-fries, and they are also used in noodle and rice dishes. They seldom need trimming. Large ones should be torn, rather than cut into pieces. The soft texture becomes rubbery if they are overcooked, so always add them to dishes at the last moment. Buy oyster mushrooms that smell and look fresh, avoiding any with

### Dried Mushrooms

Many varieties of mushrooms are available dried. They have a rich, intense flavour and are a useful store-cupboard (pantry) standby. Once they have been soaked and rconstituted, they can be stir-fried, braised, steamed or added to soups. Dried mushrooms require longer cooking than fresh ones.

To reconstitute dried mushrooms, soak them in boiling water for 20–30 minutes, depending on the size and variety of the mushoom, until tender. Drain and rinse well to remove any grit or dirt.

damp, slimy patches and discolouring. Store in a paper bag in the vegetable compartment of the refrigerator, and use as soon as possible after purchase. They do not keep for more than 2–3 days.

### Chinese black mushrooms

Sometimes known as Chinese shiitake, these pungent mushrooms are usually sold dried. Light brown in colour with white markings on the surface, they have thick-fleshed caps which can grow to about 5cm/2in in diameter and have a meaty flavour and a chewy texture.

*Above: Chinese black mushrooms are sold dried or canned.*

Once softened in warm water for about 30 minutes, the stems are removed and the caps are added to stews, stir-fries and fillings. Chinese black mushrooms are available in Asian supermarkets.

### PULSES

Used in both sweet and savoury dishes, pulses are a mainstay of the cuisine.

### Red beans

Dried red beans, also called aduki beans, are some of the smallest pulses available. In Indonesia, they are usually soaked, boiled and mashed as a stuffing for sweet cakes. They are often boiled and used as a sweet base in a dessert, sold by hawkers or from dessert stalls. They are also cooked as a sweet drink with rock sugar or sweet winter melon slices as a favourite after-meal drink.

### Beansprouts

Ubiquitous throughout Asia and China, beansprouts can be eaten raw but are usually added to stir-fried noodles for their crunch. The most common sprouts come from mung beans and soya beans. They are similar in appearance, except the soya bean at the head of the sprout is almost twice the size at about 2cm/¾in long.

The stems of both are white, but soya bean heads are pale green, while those of mung beans are yellow. Soya beans are sturdier and stronger in flavour, whereas mung beans are delicate and watery. Both types are nutritious, rich in vitamins and minerals.

Fresh sprouts can be stored in the refrigerator for up to 2–3 days. Packets of mung beansprouts are available in most supermarkets. Soya beansprouts can be found in Asian stores and some health stores.

### Soya beans

These yellow beans are about twice the size of corn kernels and play a big role in the Chinese-influenced kitchens of Indonesia, apart from the obvious soy sauce. Fermented and made into yellow bean paste, soya beans are the basis of many sauces. Sweetened with palm sugar (jaggery), they are a popular dessert and drink ingredient.

Soya beans are extremely dense and need to be soaked for 12 hours before cooking, but once cooked they are easily digested. They are very bland, however, and need plenty of robust ingredients with distinctive flavours cooking alongside them.

*Below: Beansprouts are a widely used ingredient in stir-fries.*

## ORIENTAL GREENS

Versatile and full of nutrients, oriental greens are very popular in both cuisines.

### Pak choi (Bok choy)

This perennial, green, leafy cabbage is popular throughout Asia. The ribbed, white stems are juicy and crunchy; the dark green leaves are succulent and tasty. The tender stems of small cabbages are rarely eaten raw but often stir-fried with prawns (shrimp) or added to noodles. The leaves, which are

*Above: Pak choi is excellent in stir-fry dishes as well as salads.*

mostly composed of water, require little cooking and lose a lot of volume in the process. It is a good idea to cook the leaves and stems separately, as the stems take slightly longer. These fresh greens are available in Asian stores and supermarkets.

### Chinese leaves (Chinese cabbage)

Often confused with the above, there are almost as many names for this member of the brassica family as there are ways of cooking it. In the West, it is generally called Chinese leaves, but it is also known as Chinese cabbage, Napa cabbage (mainly in the USA) and sometimes celery cabbage. In Indonesia the names for pak choi tend to be used for this vegetable, which is available all year.

Chinese leaves have a delicate sweet aroma with a mild cabbage flavour that becomes even more subtle when it is cooked. The white stalk becomes less crunchy when cooked. It is a very versatile vegetable and it can be cooked in stir-fries, stews, soups, or eaten raw in salads. It will absorb the flavours of

any other ingredients with which it is cooked and yet retain its own characteristic taste and texture. Restaurant chefs blanch the vegetable in boiling stock, which enhances the flavour, before frying, or blanch the leaves to soften them for wrapping around minced (ground) pork and fish as a festive dish. Chinese leaves can be stored for up to 10 days in the refrigerator. Don't worry if there are tiny black specks on the leaves. This is normal and will not affect the flavour.

### Mustard greens

Also known as Chinese cabbage, mustard greens look a bit like a head of lettuce such as cos or romaine, except that the leaves wrapping the heart are thick. The leaves are sharp and robust in flavour but, once blanched, they lose some of their bitterness. A classic stir-fry addition when poached with egg white and crab meat, fresh mustard greens are available in Asian markets and will keep for several days in the salad compartment of a refrigerator.

### Preserved mustard greens

In Indonesia, salty preserved mustard greens are as common as the fresh variety. They are eaten with many Indonesian seafood curries, or sliced and added to soups or omelettes. They are available in Asian markets, usually canned or vacuum-packed.

*Above: Mustard greens are larger and curlier than pak choi.*

### Water convolvulus

Also called water spinach, swamp cabbage or water morning glory, this attractive leafy green vegetable is traditionally grown in swamps or ponds, near rivers and canals, although it does grow on dry land too. In Indonesia it is essential in the spicy salad called rujak, and is often added to spiced fish or prawns and wrapped in banana leaves for steaming or barbecuing. Somewhat rare in the West, water convolvulus is occasionally available in some Asian markets and supermarkets. It is highly perishable and must be used promptly.

### Preparing water convolvulus

**1** Slit the hollow stalks right down their length to check for creepy-crawlies! Separate them from the leaves and split lengthways.

**2** Trim off the end bits that usually have a few rootlets. Slice into 7.5cm/3in pieces.

**3** Tear off leafy stems or cut into similar lengths so each stem has a few leaves. Individual leaves, if they are small, tend to shrink too much when cooked. Wash and drain thoroughly before cooking. Store refrigerated in a plastic bag for up to 2 days.

## TUBERS AND AQUATIC ROOTS

These vegetables are quite unlike root vegetables used in Western cuisine.

### Cassava (Tapioca)

Also known as manioc or tapioca, cassava is a large tuber similar in shape to a sweet potato, but longer, with skin like firm brown bark. The creamy-coloured flesh of the root is starchy and often used for sweet, sticky puddings such kueh bengka. Cassava can be steamed and tossed with desiccated (dry unsweetened shredded) coconut or simply eaten as a sweet snack, or mashed and sweetened with palm sugar (jaggery) and coconut milk as a baked pudding. It has a subtly sweet, almost buttery flavour, sometimes with nuances of almond and new potato. Cassava must never be eaten raw. Fresh cassava tubers are available in Asian markets.

### Tapioca flour

This silky flour is made from the starch of the cassava root. Primarily, it is used to thicken sauces and desserts, but it is also used to make fresh rice papers. The flour is available in Asian stores.

### Mooli (Daikon)

Apart from being white, this vegetable looks very similar to a large carrot. Also known as Oriental white radish, or mooli in Hindi, it is crisp and juicy with a slightly fiery edge. It can be eaten raw or cooked and it is a popular vegetable throughout Indonesia. They can be eaten raw, pickled or stir-fried. Daikon can be found in Asian markets.

### Jicama

Resembling a large turnip, this root vegetable has a delicate sweet taste with a crunchy texture, similar to water chestnut. Simply peel before use and cut into chunks or slices for soups, salads and stir-fries. Jicamas can be found in most Asian stores.

### Lotus root and seeds

The lotus plant, or water lily, with its delicate flowers, is quite unique, and edible in its entirety. The stamens are infused to make a fragrant tea; the seeds are dried and boiled for use in festive sweets and cakes; the large leaves are used for wrapping sticky rice and steamed snacks; the stems are peeled, sliced and added to salads, soups and braised dishes. Lotus roots are tan-coloured with a pinkish hue. The roots taste similar to water chestnuts. When sliced, they reveal small holes which hold the seeds. Chinese tradition says that the nourishing lotus root aids blood circulation and increases virility. The roots, stems and seeds of the lotus plant are available, fresh, dried and preserved, in most Asian stores. If dried, all of them need to be soaked overnight before being cooked.

*Above: The texture of a jicama is like a cross between an apple and a potato.*

*Above: Fresh lotus roots, which are in fact rhizomes, look like linked sausages. The papery leaves and light-coloured seeds are also widely used.*

### Taro

This root vegetable, known as taro or yam is either small and egg-shaped or about 13cm/5in long and barrel-shaped. Both varieties have short hairs and white purple-flecked flesh. The larger variety is firm with a nutty flavour; the smaller is creamier and sweeter.

Taro roots are available in Asian stores as well as in some supermarkets. Indonesian cooking also features the tender stalks of young taro for curries. They absorb the flavour and sauce of the dish.

*Below: Taro is a rough-skinned tuber.*

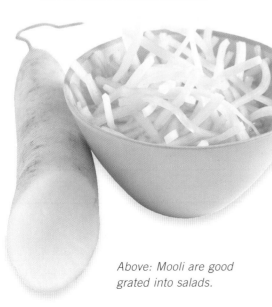

*Above: Mooli are good grated into salads.*

# FRUIT

Traditionally, fruit is eaten at the end of a meal to cleanse the palate or aid the digestion, while desserts and cakes are nibbled and indulged in as snacks.

### BANANAS

The banana plant looks like a tree but is actually a perennial herb. Every year, it grows a new 'trunk' and, after it has borne blossom and fruit, it dies back to its roots. The fruit grows in bunches (hands). Most are yellow-skinned and pale-fleshed, but there are some with orange flesh and others with green-striped skins and pink flesh. The sweetest tend to be short and stubby.

After coconuts, bananas are possibly the most widely used fruit in Indonesia. They even have grand names like Baston or Cavendish, and these are exported around the world. Latundan is flattish with white flesh; Lacatan is long and slender with sweet yellow flesh; Senorita is one of the smallest at 8cm/3in, and the Saba is like a plantain and has to be cooked. In Indonesia, a favourite snack is pisang goreng (battered and fried bananas) or jemput jemput, mashed bananas mixed with rice flour and fried. Many desserts call for bananas, fresh or fried, while a number of savoury dishes require the leaves or blossom of the banana plant.

### Banana leaves

You don't need foil, baking parchment or clear film (plastic wrap) when you've got banana leaves. They can be used as plates, table mats or be shaped into

*Below: Banana leaves are useful for wrapping food.*

*Above: The purple banana blossom may be eaten as a vegetable.*

bowls and cups. The leaves are often used as wrappings for pâtés and sweet and savoury sticky rice cakes. Banana leaves are available in Asian and African supermarkets, sold both fresh and frozen.

### Banana blossom

The lovely deep purple flower of the banana tree is enjoyed throughout South-east Asia as a vegetable, especially in Indonesian salads. Only the inner yellow blossoms are used; they are fabulous sliced, blanched and tossed with coconut cream, cooked prawns (shrimp) and chilli and shrimp paste sambal. To prepare the inner blossom, slice it finely and soak in water with a squeeze of lemon or lime juice to prevent it discolouring. The blossoms can be eaten raw but have a slightly bitter taste. The purple outer husks are inedible.

### COCONUT

The coconut is the most commonly used fruit for both sweet and savoury dishes throughout Indonesia – indeed, throughout all of tropical Asia. Ripe fruits are hulled, shredded and squeezed for a clear white milk that is essential in Indonesian curries. The soft, jelly-like flesh of the young nuts makes a tasty snack or forms a sweet base for tropical drinks.

*Above: The brown, hairy stone of the coconut contains the water and flesh.*

Coconut palm leaves are woven into baskets and mats, or used to wrap rice for boiling and serving with satay. The spines are cut into lengths for satay skewers, and the husks and fibres are used as mattress stuffing, fuel, or for making ropes.

The whole coconut that we buy is only the stone (pit) of the actual fruit; the husk and fibres are removed in the country of origin. When buying a coconut, the hard shell should be brown and hairy. Shake it and you should hear the sound of the coconut water inside. To extract this liquid, pierce the eyes on top of the coconut and pour it out. The coconut water should be clear and taste sweet. It is generally drunk or used to tenderize meat. Once you have extracted the water, place the coconut on a flat surface and use a heavy object like a cleaver or hammer to hit it all the way round. Pull the shell apart, pry the flesh out with a knife, and peel the brown skin off the flesh so that it is ready to use. If you have difficulty cracking the coconut, place it in a fairly hot oven for about 15 minutes, until it cracks. The flesh is often easier to extract from the shell using this method.

### Coconut milk

This is the equivalent of dairy cream in Asia, and fundamental in most curries and puddings. It is used to enrich sauces and soups, especially in Indonesian cooking. Coconut milk is also boiled with red or green beans, bananas and mangoes, and sweetened with palm sugar (jaggery) for a popular dessert called penghat in Indonesia.

When you squeeze coconut flesh without water, you get an initial cream called 'first milk' that is used for desserts. The second milk comes from adding a little warm water to yield a thinner liquid, used mainly in curries. (If thin coconut milk is allowed to settle in a bowl, a little cream will rise to the top, and may be skimmed off for use.)

Fresh coconut milk does not keep well and is usually made daily. It can turn rancid very quickly in hot weather and is best refrigerated if you are not using it immediately. It keeps for up to 2 days if chilled.

Canned coconut milk is now widely available, and you can purchase powder or blocks of cream from Asian markets, health stores and supermarkets. These are essential store-cupboard items for enthusiasts of South-east Asian cuisine. Follow the package instructions for use.

### Coconut oil

By boiling coconut cream gently until the liquid evaporates, coconut oil is made. The oil is used by Indonesians for rich curries but is a saturated fat that turns solid very quickly.

*Below: Red-skinned mangoes are eaten as a fruit or in desserts, and green-skinned ones as a vegetable.*

### Green coconut water

The coconut water used for cooking is extracted from young, green coconuts. Mild and sweet, it is used in a number of braised dishes and cakes. Although you can use the coconut water from ripened coconuts, it is best to look in Asian markets for a young coconut. It will be cylindrical in shape with a conical top and a white, spongy shell, as the green outer skin will have been removed.

### MANGO

Originally from India, the mango is much loved in Indonesia. The sweetest varieties are thick, round and tapered at one end. The skins are yellow, pale orange or green depending on the type, and ripened ones are eaten mainly as a fruit. There are also green mangoes that never change colour and are used mainly as salad vegetables when sliced finely or shredded. Imported mangoes from India and Thailand are available all year round. The sweet, juicy, yellow or orange flesh is thirst-quenching, with a delightful aroma of pine, and is a good source of vitamin A. Different types of mango are widely available. To eat mango, cut a slice from the side and score the flesh into squares, then invert the skin and slice cubes of flesh away from the rind.

Ripe mangoes are rich in vitamins, especially A and C, and are a good source of betacarotene.

### Making coconut milk

While most wet markets sell grated coconut for making milk, or cans of milk, it is easy to make.

**1** Grate the flesh from a fresh ripened coconut, or shred it in a food processor.

**2** Put the grated flesh into a bowl and knead thoroughly. Squeeze out the creamy 'first milk'.

**3** Pour roughly 600ml/1 pint/ 2½ cups warm water over the shreds. Stir and leave to steep for 30 minutes.

**4** Line a sieve (strainer) with muslin (cheesecloth) over a bowl and ladle the coconut into it.

**5** Gather the muslin tightly in your hands and squeeze out any excess liquid. This is the 'second milk'.

## DURIAN

This large fruit, encased in a spiky armour-like skin, is creamy, dense and pungent. If you can put up with the strong, cheesy odour, the delicious yellow flesh has nut and honey overtones, quite unlike any other fruit, and is considered an aphrodisiac. Durian is a much sought-after fruit during the season, from May to October. It is an expensive fruit and only available in some Asian markets. The best ones come from Malaysia and have butter-soft flesh with a slight bitter edge. Thai durians tend to be woody and dry. Avoid any fruits that have split.

### Preparing durian

Using a wooden wedge that has a thin, tapered end, force it down along each natural ridge between the rows of spikes. The prickly shell will split open easily to reveal large seeds coated in pulp. The pulp can be tugged, or sucked and licked clean from the large seeds. If not eaten straight away, freeze the durian flesh in air-tight containers so as not to impart its strong smell to other foods.

## JACKFRUIT

Large and spiky, jackfruits look similar to durian but have short stubs instead of spikes. When sliced open, a jackfruit reveals a cluster of yellow fruit, each encircling a large seed. The texture is delightfully crunchy and the taste is similar to ripe mango.

There are two distinct types: nangka, which can weigh in at 5kg/11lb and grow as large as two rugby balls, and chempedak, which is widely grown in Indonesia. The taste of chempedak is more fragrant, with nuances of pineapple and apricot, and the flesh is creamy and chewy at the same time. Packed with vitamins, jackfruit is enjoyed on its

*Above: Jackfruit is large and plentiful. It features in many popular savoury and sweet dishes.*

own as well as mixed with other fruits in tropical fruit salad. Peel the fruit like a pineapple, pull away the fruits attached to a central stalk and they separate easily. Eat the flesh and reserve the seeds, which can be boiled or roasted and eaten as a snack. Peeled, whole, canned green jackfruit are available in some Asian markets.

*Below: Knobbly kalamansi limes are widely used in South-east Asian cuisine.*

## LIME

Fresh green limes are used for their juice, much like lemons in Mediterranean cooking, or pickled and dried for use in sambals and chutneys. Tossed in marinades and dressings, they impart a slightly fragrant, citrus taste. Kaffir limes yield aromatic lime leaves integral to Indonesian cooking. The rough-textured rind is grated and added to many savoury dishes. The fruit is highly prized in sambals and curries. Both varieties and the kaffir lime leaves are available in Asian markets.

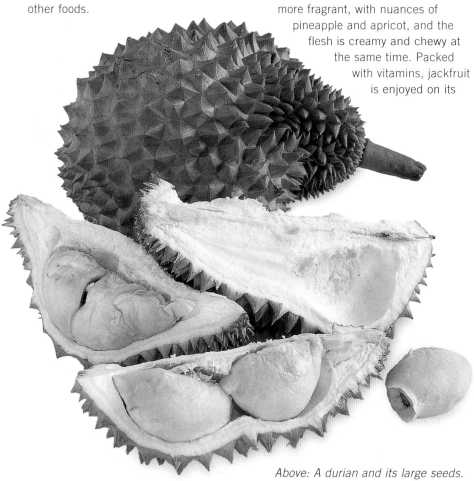

*Above: A durian and its large seeds.*

*Above: Lychees are best eaten raw.*

## LYCHEE AND LONGAN

Both lychees and longans are native to the sub-tropical regions of South-east Asia, and they require heat and high humidity to ripen well. They belong to the same family, although the smaller and less fleshy longan is sometimes regarded as the inferior relative. Lychees have terracotta-pink, bumpy skins, rather than the smooth, brown ones of longans, but both are easily peeled to reveal gleaming white, occasionally pink, juicy flesh covering a shiny, coffee-coloured seed. Clusters of fresh lychees and longans are sold on their stalks in the markets and supermarkets of Asia. Sweet and fragrant, they are usually eaten as a refreshing snack. Fresh longans can be found in some Asian markets, and lychees are readily available in Asian markets and most supermarkets. They keep well in the refrigerator and are delicious chilled. Lychees and longans are also sold in cans, preserved in their own juice or in syrup.

## PAPAYA

This ripe, yellow-skinned fruit, with its sweet, flame-coloured flesh, is also known as paw paw. It is full of vitamins and honey-sweet. When a savoury recipe calls for papaya, it is a different variety that is required. Large and round, or pear-shaped, this papaya has a dark green skin with pale green flesh and white seeds. High in iron, this tart fruit is enjoyed as a vegetable, peeled and finely sliced, or shredded, in salads. Both types of papaya can be found in Asian markets. Choose fruit with firm, unblemished skin, not bruised or shrivelled. Ripe papayas do not last very long. Slit them open, scoop out the seeds and enjoy the flesh with a squeeze of fresh lime.

## PINEAPPLE

Grown throughout tropical regions, pineapples vary in size, juiciness and sweetness. Often pineapple slices are sold with a little salt and chilli powder to sprinkle on them. Ripe pineapples are mainly eaten as a fruit, but are an important ingredient in Indonesian sour curries, especially with fish and shellfish. Pineapples are readily available; when choosing, look for a firm, puckered skin, with a good orange colouring and a good fragrance.

*Above: Pineapples come in a variety of different sizes.*

## Preparing pineapple

To prepare fresh pineapple slices, first slice off the leaves, then use a sharp or serrated knife to cut off the skin in vertical strips about 1cm/½in thick. Make diagonal cuts all along the fruit, removing any black eyes. Slice the whole fruit lengthways into four quarters and remove the hard, pithy core. Finally, cube or slice and serve.

*Above: Rambutans have a distinctive skin covered in soft spiky hairs. They are available fresh or prepared in cans.*

## RAMBUTAN

Shaggy-haired rambutans look like tiny red sea urchins. There are a number of varieties, varying in sweetness and coloured with streaks of gold, orange or green. The hairy shells are easy to open and encase a translucent white fruit with a stone (pit) in the middle, similar to the lychee and longan. Cool and sweet, these fruits are available in some Asian markets.

## STAR FRUIT

Also known as carambola, this pretty fruit is mildly floral tasting and similar in texture to an Asian pear but juicier. With a smooth shiny skin, the fruit has an attractive star shape when sliced through the centre. In both countries, the ripened yellow fruit is enjoyed as a snack or pulped for its refreshing juice. The green immature fruit is sliced finely and served as a tangy vegetable, salted and dried as a pickle ingredient, or tossed in salads. Star fruit is available in some Asian markets and from good supermarkets.

## SOUR STAR FRUIT

These small, sour fruit, also known as belimbing, are related to the carambola that grows profusely all over Indonesia. Found widely in high altitude regions, it is variously called camia, cucumber tree and tree sorrel. The thumb-sized fruits grow in clusters and impart a zesty, tangy flavour to seafood curries and salads. The leaves are crunchy with a faint bitter edge. They are not widely available in the West, but may be found in markets that specialize in South-east Asian ingredients. Otherwise young spinach leaves may be substituted.

### How to prepare sour star fruit (belimbing) pickle

**1** Remove the small stalks at the ends of the fruit. Remove the pith.

**2** Cut up the fruits or mash lightly until you get a coarse paste.

**3** Sprinkle liberally with salt and set aside to sweat for an hour.

**4** Using a square of muslin (cheesecloth), squeeze out the moisture and toss with two chopped red chillies, 5ml/1 tsp sugar and 15ml/1 tbsp vinegar.

**5** Sprinkle with 30ml/2 tbsp chopped nuts and serve as a relish.

*Below: Sapodilla, with its orange, fuzzy skin, looks similar to an apricot.*

## SAPODILLA

These kiwi-fruit sized fruit originate from Central America but are widely grown in Indonesia. Variously called chiko or chiku, they have a light, slightly fuzzy skin that when peeled reveals a soft, tan flesh with black pips. The flesh is luscious like a soft pear and tastes of burnt sugar. Sapodillas are available from some Asian grocers and markets.

## GUAVA

A native of Brazil, the guava was taken by the Portuguese to the Philippines in the 17th century, and gradually spread across the tropical countries. It is grown widely in Indonesia and there is a profusion of different types, which may be round, ovoid or pear-shaped, and weigh from 25–350g/1–12oz. The thick outer skin ranges from white to pale green, pink or red; the flesh may be white, yellow or pink and contain many small seeds. Guavas have a sweet aroma ranging from rose blossom to mango, and are eaten mainly as a dessert fruit. They are available from most Thai and Indian markets and some supermarkets.

## MANGOSTEEN

Grown mainly in hot, humid tropical countries, mangosteens are virtually unknown outside tropical Asia. The handsome fruits are like large berries, the size of apples, with a smooth, rich-looking, red-purple thick rind, partially covered with the flower sepals that remain attached as the fruit ripens. Inside the rind the pulp is chalky white and divided into five to seven segments. The large segments contain a seed but the smaller segments are seedless. The flesh has a delicious perfume. Mangosteens are eaten as dessert fruit.

## SOURSOP

Often mistaken for durian, soursops are grown widely in humid tropical countries. The fruits may weigh as much as 3kg/8lb, and are borne on thick, woody stalks. The thick skin is dark green with rows of soft green stubby spikes – hence the durian comparison. The fruit is very soft, white and creamy and very juicy, ranging from tart to sweet flavours. Buried within the flesh are many shiny, black seeds. A rich source of vitamin C, they are often puréed for the juice. They are available in South-east Asian and Chinese markets.

## CUSTARD APPLE

Originating from tropical America, the custard apple was introduced to the region by the Portuguese via Madagascar. It thrives in lowland tropics and sub-tropics and is known as a nona kapri in Malaysia. This means the 'nona from Africa', borrowing from the botanical name *Anona longifolia*. The fruits are heart-shaped, buff or green in colour, and each about 10cm/4in in diameter. The skin is thin and may have small bumps depending on the variety. The creamy white flesh surrounds a fibrous central core. Small black seeds are embedded in the flesh, which has a custard-like consistency and is slightly astringent, but sweet when ripe. It is readily available in Indian and South-east Asian stores and markets.

*Above: Mangosteens have a white flesh with a delicate flavour and are best eaten raw.*

# TOFU

Far from a 'poor man's meat', tofu or soy beancurd is enjoyed globally today, and stirred up into great tastes by Indonesian cooks. Protein-rich and low in calories, tofu is devoid of cholesterol. It also provides essential amino acids, vitamins and minerals for good health. It is made by combining soya bean milk with a coagulant such as gypsum powder to form curds which are then pressed together into blocks. Some find it too bland, but this very quality makes tofu great for absorbing other flavours. The firmer type can be added to stir-fries, and when fried it has a wonderful texture. It may also be used as a container for various stuffings, and adds healthy bulk to soups, braised vegetarian dishes and spring roll fillings.

*Above, clockwise from top: Fried, silken and firm tofu, all varying in degrees of firmness and suited to stir-fries or soups.*

## FRESH TOFU

Soft white blocks of fresh tofu are packed in water and are available in most Asian markets. The UHT varieties in cartons are also available in many supermarkets and come in two types – soft or firm. Generally, the soft silken texture is better for soups and steamed dishes, whereas the firm variety is best in stir-fries and fillings. Tofu is best used immediately, but, if it is kept submerged in water that is changed daily, it can be stored for 3–4 days in the refrigerator.

*Above: Cubes of fermented tofu.*

## PRESERVED TOFU

Cubes of fresh tofu can be preserved in salty water or brine for several months. Before use the tofu should be thoroughly rinsed in water and drained. Used sparingly (because of their strong taste), cubes of preserved tofu add extra flavour to stir-fries and other vegetable and meat dishes. Preserved tofu can be found in most Asian stores.

## FRIED TOFU

Made by deep-frying firm tofu until a brown skin forms, this is used in many dishes and salads, and as an alternative to meat. It has a delicious, slightly chewy texture and a flavour rather similar to omelette. The Indonesian iconic dishes of tahu goreng and gado gado feature fried tofu prominently. Both are dressed with shredded vegetables and bathed in a rich, spicy peanut sauce. The tofu absorbs the flavour of the sauce well and retains its firm texture.

## TOFU SKINS

These are made by lifting the skin as soy milk is boiled and drying it flat to form brown, wrinkly sheets. The skins are often used in manufacturing vegetarian meat substitutes, as the texture is very similar to cooked meat. If the skins have been stored for any time, they tend to become stiff and crack easily when handled. If this happens, they have to be moistened slightly with a damp towel before being used as spring roll wrappers. Many Indonesian and Filipino spring rolls are made with tofu skin as a festive wrapper.

## TOFU WAFERS

Light brown pieces of slightly sweetened, dried tofu can be fried to make a 'crackling' to top stir-fried noodles or add to vegetable stews. In Indonesian cooking, such garnishes are an extremely important feature – often giving a dish its essential flavour or texture.

# FISH AND SHELLFISH

The coastal waters off the Indonesian archipelago are alive with a variety of tropical seafood. Indonesia also blessed with a network of river systems that start from the mountain ranges and run through the jungles to finally join the sea. In every town and village, there are usually wet markets that include fishmongers selling absolutely fresh fish.

Fish is an important source of protein, vitamins and amino acids. Calcium is also plentiful in small fish such as anchovies and sprats. Most coastal communities depend more on fish than meat for their daily diet.

Fish market stall holders traditionally bought their fish at the crack of dawn from fishermen, straight from the fishing boats. These days, this practice is more organized and buying from large fish wholesalers is the norm.

Much seafood ends up in noodle dishes; Indonesian laksas all feature seafood prominently. Up until the 1950s, refrigeration was rare and all fish bought had to be cooked on the same day. This still applies in many rural areas in Indonesia, and has trained the local tastebuds to expect extremely fresh ocean produce.

## CARP

A powerful swimmer, the carp leaps like a salmon and migrates in shoals. There are numerous species of carp, all of which have different names. Not all

*Below: Carp is one of the hardiest of all fish, and has meaty flesh that varies in taste according to how it is cooked. It is often wrapped in banana leaves and steamed with herbs.*

*Below: Fresh catfish is versatile and easy to use. It is often sold on Indonesian street stalls, grilled and served with vegetables.*

carp are good to eat, as some feed in shallow, muddy waters which can affect the taste. The common variety in Indonesia is known as ikan mas, and is bred in areas including West Java and South Sumatra. It is only eaten fresh, never dried, and is sometimes sold live at the wet market in plastic bags filled with water.

## CATFISH

Primarily freshwater fish, catfish are so called because of their barbels, used for feeling along the river beds, which look like whiskers. Free of scales and small bones, catfish are easy to prepare, but the quality of their flesh varies as they are bottom feeders and feed off live and dead prey. In Indonesia, deep-fried catfish is popular, particularly at food stalls, where it is served with a spicy sauce made from chillies, peanuts and tomatoes, in a dish called pecel lele.

## EEL

Adult eels are at their plumpest when they have turned silver with almost black backs. Females weigh three times as much as males, so a female silver eel is highly prized. Eels should be bought alive, as they go off quickly once dead. Ask the fishmonger to kill and skin them for you and to chop them into 5cm/2in lengths. Eel can be fried and served with a simple sauce, or poached. If grilling (broiling), marinate it first.

## HERRING

While the common name is herring, these fish are also known as sprat or rainbow sardine. Generally growing to about 15cm/6in, with a dark green back and silver belly, they have very fine bones. Like all oily fish, herring must be absolutely fresh or they will taste rancid. As herrings contain numerous bones, you might ask the fishmonger to bone or fillet them for you. They can be gutted either through the belly or through the gills, leaving the roe inside. Herring are extremely tasty when fried and eaten with a chilli dip. Larger herrings can be gutted and filleted before cooking. Their oiliness makes herrings ideal for grilling (broiling) and barbecuing. Score the fish on both sides to ensure even cooking.

*Above: Milkfish is hugely popular in Indonesia.*

*Above: Sea bass has a delicate taste that works well with herbs and spices.*

*Above: Snappers have a delicate flavour and are usually cooked in curries.*

### MILKFISH

Generally about 1m/3ft in length, with a symmetrical shape, the milkfish (known locally as bangas) is an extremely important fish in Indonesia. It is farmed extensively. Young milkfish live at sea for two to three weeks and then migrate to fresh and brackish water before returning to the sea for reproduction. They are collected from rivers and raised in ponds, then sold fresh, frozen, canned or smoked. In taste and texture the milk fish is similar to sea bass or mullet.

### RED GROUPER

Red grouper are farmed and caught wild. They have bright orange skin with uneven spotting.The pure white flesh has a good texture and flavour, and the fish has become very sought after and expensive. Generally the fish are over 1m/3ft in length. They are usually sold live, or very fresh, at wet markets.

### SEA BASS

A fine fish, sea bass have variable but always striking coloration, from silvery to light brown to orange with large-edged blue spots. They have a sleek shape rather like a salmon, and can grow to a length of 90cm/36in and weigh up to 7kg/15½lb. The white flesh is firm and

delicately flavoured and tastes best when simply steamed. Sea bass is a versatile fish, it have very few bones and the firm flesh holds well during cooking. It can be grilled (broiled), baked, braised, shallow-fried, steamed or even poached whole. Look out for bright, silvery skin and clear eyes.

### SNAKEHEAD

This eel-like fish is highly prized for its meaty flesh and full flavour, and features in Cantonese fish and rice vermicelli soup (yue tau mifun). The fish are usually sold live. They have a near-black, slippery skin and are often mistaken for fat eels. They are popular in curries, grilled (broiled), fried or flaked for relishes.

### SNAPPER

One of the most important groups of local fish, snappers are highly esteemed and easily recognized by their straight ventral profile with pointed snout. These snap when they are caught, hence their name. Most are brightly coloured, ranging from deep red in the larger species to shocking pink, silver and yellow, usually with lines and spots. Snappers can be baked, grilled (broiled), poached, steamed or pan-fried whole.

### STINGRAY

Although the normal variety is relatively small, about 30cm/12in across its widest part, stingrays can also grow to enormous size, weighing as much as 200kg/450lb. They may be coloured from sandy to dark brown, or marked with numerous spots, but a better recognition point is their whip-like tail. Grilled or fried, they have a similar flavour and texture to skate.

### THREADFIN/TASSEL FISH

Probably the most expensive fish and quite rare, these fish have a delicate sweet flesh reminiscent of cod or halibut. They are large, up to 120cm/4ft long, and are mostly sold as steaks or cutlets. They are silvery-green above with a creamy belly and the name refers to the four threads on each pectoral fin.

### WOLF HERRING/DORAB

Specimens up to 60cm/24in long have been caught in deep waters off Asian coasts but the market variety is usually around 45cm/18in long. The fish has a bluish-green back with silvery sides that go grey when it has been dead a while. The large upturned mouth looks fierce but the flesh has a sweet flavour, and the numerous bones cannot spoil the excellent taste and flaky texture.

## SQUID

Along with octopus and cuttlefish, squid are members of the cephalopod family. Torpedo-shaped and flanked by two fins, eight short and two long tentacles, the entire body is edible and enjoyed throughout the region. Squid is easy to prepare and can be cooked in a variety of ways, such as stir-fried with spices.

### Preparing squid

**1** Check the squid is fresh and intact. Rinse it well in fresh water.

**2** Grip the head in one hand, the body in the other, and tug the head out of the body sac, pulling most of the innards with it. Grip the top of the backbone and pull it out. Rinse the inside of the sac and pat dry.

**3** Sever the arms and tentacles from the head and innards and put beside the sac. Discard the rest, including the skin.

If stir-frying squid, slit the prepared sac from top to bottom and turn it inside out. Flatten it on a board and score the inside surface lightly with a knife, pressing just hard enough to make a crisscross pattern. Cut lengthways into ribbons, which will curl when cooked briefly.

## CRAB

Whenever possible, Indonesians enjoy lobster and crab, including the meaty blue crab found off Palawan. However, due to the expense, lobster and crab are often reserved for special occasions, when they are steamed with oyster sauce, or deep-fried and served with a chilli sambal.

There are several varieties of crab, the most common being mottled or flower crabs, named on account of the pale blue mottling on their shells. They are about the size of an adult palm, smaller than the large grey mud crabs. They make very good eating, especially in the well-loved Singapore dish of chilli crab.

*Above: The blue mottled crab is popular in Indonesia, and has plenty of meat.*

### Preparing crab

Usually sold live, crabs tend to become comatose when chilled for a few hours. Make sure the crab is dry, with no sign of water sloshing around in the shell, which should be firm and contain no cracks or holes. Turn the crab belly up and remove the soft V-shaped flap on the belly. Pull the top shell off, scoop out the soft, yellowish coral and reserve. Discard the feathery gills and snap off the legs and claws. The larger claws

*Above: Prawn tails turn salmon-pink when they are cooked. The shells must be removed before they are eaten.*

should be cracked but not entirely broken, so the flesh can be easily extracted when cooked. Rinse the body and cut into two or more pieces. Alternatively, steam the crabs whole until they turn deep pink throughout.

## PRAWNS (SHRIMP)

In spite of the abundance, most of the prawns (shrimp) and squid that are caught in Indonesian waters go to international markets as they are too expensive for locals to afford. However, the tiny shrimp that are not exported are very cheap and are sold in vast quantities in the local markets, destined for a delicious dish of nasi goreng (Indonesian fried rice) or stir-fried water spinach (kangkung). They are also fermented and dried to make the pungent shrimp paste, terasi, which is added to many spice pastes and sambals. In South Sumatra and Kalimantan, the locals enjoy a regular supply of large, juicy river prawns which are often chargrilled with spices.

Prawns have a sweet flavour and turn pink or orange when they are cooked. Buy fresh raw prawns if possible, choosing specimens that are a translucent grey colour tinged with blue. Juicy and meaty, the bigger prawns are often grilled (broiled) whole, or added to stir-fries and curries; the small ones are dried and added to stocks to enhance the flavour. The small freshwater ones are more delicate and are often steamed briefly, or cooked live in the famous dish called drunken prawns.

*Above: Gigantic gigas oysters are now rare in the waters off Indonesia, due to over-harvesting.*

## SAND LOBSTER

The sand lobster looks like an immature lobster, and has a broad head and tiny claws. Most of the meat is contained within the body section and has much the same delicate, luxurious flavour as normal lobster. When sand lobsters are plentiful, cooks often use them in place of prawns for spiced or steamed seafood dishes.

## MOLLUSCS

Freshly caught molluscs are always sold live and deteriorate rapidly, so cook them as soon as possible after buying. When you are shopping for bivalves such as mussels, clams and oysters, check that they contain sea water and feel heavy for their size. Do not buy any that have broken or gaping shells. When you give them a sharp tap, they should snap shut. If they don't, discard them immediately. Molluscs must be eaten within a day of purchase, but will keep for a few hours in the refrigerator. Put them in a bowl, cover with a damp cloth and keep them in the coldest part of the refrigerator (at 2°C/36°F) until use.

## Cockles

These small bivalves are very popular at seafood stalls and are simply boiled and eaten with pungent chilli and vinegar sauces. They may contain mud and sand but they will expel this if left

*Right: Cockles and mussels are popular bivalves that are farmed and caught wild in Indonesia.*

overnight in a bucket of sea water or salted water. Those with paler flesh are said to taste better than those with dark flesh, so look for cockles with pale shells. They can be eaten raw or boiled. They are good steamed, stewed with tomatoes and onions and made into soup. Cockles can be added to rice and other seafood dishes.

## Mussels

These are either green-lipped or brown with a pale yellow flesh. They are simply steamed or cooked in Chinese wine with garlic and ginger. When buying mussels, allow 450g/1lb per person, as the shells make up much of the weight.

## Oysters

Mainly imported from Australia or New Zealand, oysters are more of a Western treat in upmarket seafood places. Those used in omelettes are a smaller variety, or barnacles are sometimes used instead. Oysters can be kept for a couple of days, thanks to the sea water contained in their shells. Store them cupped side down. Never store shellfish in fresh water, or they will die. Ready-frozen bivalves should not be kept in the freezer for more than 2 months.

## Scallops

Served steamed with ginger and garlic, scallops make an elegant appetizer. As an exception to the rule about buying fresh molluscs, scallops are often sold already opened and cleaned.

---

**Preparing molluscs**

**1** Keep the molluscs covered with a damp cloth in the refrigerator until ready to use.

**2** Scrub under cold water, using a stiff brush to remove any grit.

**3** Tap each shell sharply with a knife. Discard any that do not close. Cook according to recipe, discarding any molluscs that have not opened during cooking.

---

# DRIED AND FERMENTED FISH

Many Indonesian cooks still turn up their noses at store-bought stock or seasoning powders, and prefer to boil handfuls of dried shrimps, ikan bilis (sprats or anchovies), cuttlefish or dried scallops to make the requisite stock for noodles and other dishes. Small dried fish and crustaceans are by no means restricted to such a role and are also enjoyed as crunchy snacks or side dishes, chillied or spiced.

## DRIED ANCHOVIES

Commonly found in all Chinese and Thai shops, dried anchovies are integral to the cooking of Indonesia. Sold whole, generally, these finger-length fish are used as stock for seafood dishes, or fried until crispy to be served as a side dish with peanuts and coconut rice. Tossed in a rich chilli sambal, they make a delicious condiment.

*Above: Dried anchovies are often munched on as snacks.*

## DRIED PRAWNS (SHRIMP)

Originating from south India and Sri Lanka, these prized dried shellfish are used in myriad ways, notably in pastes such as Indonesian terasi. They have a rich, salty flavour and a chewy texture, and have to be soaked or boiled briefly to release their distinctive taste. Dried prawns are an important seasoning in many spice blends, especially those meant for seafood curries. They are also added to sambals and condiments. They come in many sizes, some so tiny as to look like little commas, others 2.5cm/1in long. Matt pink or light tan in

colour, they are available in all Asian markets. Stored in an airtight jar, they will keep for months.

## DRIED SQUID

An ingredient used in Indonesia, dried squid is used as a crunchy addition to Indonesian salads or soaked until soft for Chinese dishes. Grilled (broiled) or roasted, dried squid lends a smoky sweetness and a strong amber colour to soup stocks. When soaked in water with borax powder, the squid turns gelatinous and is sliced up and added to stir-fries or soups. Dried squid are available in most Chinese markets.

## SALT FISH

Different types of fish are dried and salted, but the most popular are threadfin. They are generally fried to be eaten with congee (rice porridge) by the Chinese, or added to Indonesian stews and stir-fries. Salt fish is available in Asian food markets.

## SHRIMP PASTE

Fermented shrimp paste is known as terasi in Indonesia. Terasi is a traditional condiment essential to practically all Indonesian cooking. It is made from tiny shrimp that have been salted, dried, pounded then left to ferment in the hot, humid equatorial conditions until the aroma is pungent. Shrimp paste may be bought in blocks or jars and should be kept refrigerated or in an airtight tub.

### Using dried prawns
• Used in stocks, dried prawns should be soaked in warm water for 20 minutes or briefly blanched in boiling water if needed as a salad dressing ingredient. This plumps them up and releases their flavour.
• Grind in a mortar and pestle until coarse or fine as required, then toss with lime juice and chilli paste as a pungent dip, or as a flavouring for fried rice.
• Deep-fry them and mix with sliced dried chillies as a crunchy condiment and topping.

*Above: Dried squid has a subtle fishy aroma, but a strong flavour.*

### Preparing shrimp paste
Shrimp paste can be used straight from the packet if it is to be ground with other herbs and spices and fried, but it should be toasted to temper its raw taste before using in sambals, dressings and salads.

**1** Cut off a lump of paste and shape it into a 1cm/½in cube. Mould it on to a metal skewer.

**2** Rotate the cube over a low to medium flame, or under an electric grill (broiler), until it begins to char a little along the edges. Ventilate your kitchen to let the strong smell dissipate, as it can linger.

**3** Alternatively, wrap the paste in a piece of foil and toast in a hot pan, turning occasionally, or wrap it in a small plastic bag and microwave for 20–30 seconds.

# POULTRY

As poultry is so popular in Indonesian cooking, there is a thriving commercial industry in designated areas. Chickens and ducks are bred by many rural families and smallholdings, and even in some highly urbanized areas. Many rural families will have a makeshift coop in their backyard where they rear their own chickens, ducks and geese.

In open markets throughout the regions, you can see tricycles and other makeshift modes of transport laden with live birds wending their way through villages and small towns. The dead birds are then brought home, gutted and plunged into boiling water to make the feathers easier to pull off. Small game birds such as quail and squab are also common, often spit-roasted and devoured as a snack. The eggs of all these birds are eaten in a variety of ways.

## CHICKEN

Similar to the rest of the world, chickens in the major cities of Indonesia are mostly battery-reared today, thanks to modern supermarkets and consumer demand. Free-range birds are more expensive and, apart from those bred by rural families, they do not feature much in Indonesian cuisine due to the cost. Chicken is rich in high-quality protein, providing all the amino acids required by the body. The white meat is low in fat and contains less saturated fat than other meat.

## DUCK

The rearing of ducks is largely confined to rural communities. Ducks are easy to raise, being foragers needing only table scraps and whatever insects and worms they can find in the soil. In Indonesia, ducks are not only a source of food, but their feathers and down are recycled into bedding and furnishings. Duck is confined to relatively few dishes, such as Indonesian grilled marinated duck (bebek panggang hijau) and Sumatran duck with chillies (gulai itek), and spicy stews.

## GOOSE

Although it is not a common bird in Indonesia, the Chinese, wherever they hang their hats, are past masters at cooking goose. The large bird is braised in a rich broth of soy sauce, sugar, five-spice powder and galangal. It is then sliced and served with a sharp chilli and vinegar sauce and plain rice. Geese are commercially rare and have to be ordered specially from supermarkets.

## PIGEON AND QUAIL

Small birds, such as quail and squab, are not very commonly eaten now, but quail's eggs are sold widely in Chinese stores. They usually end up in soups. They used to be popular as staple Chinese restaurant items, but have become rare. Both birds are excellent when marinated in wine and soy sauce and deep-fried.

*Above: Quail's eggs are a delicacy in the East as much as they are in the West.*

## EGGS

Almost all eggs are edible and, around the world, the eggs of all types of birds are eaten. Eggs are incredibly versatile and be cooked on their own, either boiled, poached, fried or scrambled, or combined with other ingredients to make a number of dishes. They range in colour from white to dark tan.

There is not much one can say about hens' eggs as they are so familiar. Duck eggs, on the other hand, are a delicacy and are usually available salted or as century eggs, which are a special treat eaten with pickled ginger. Chinese in origin, salted duck eggs are boiled and eaten with rice congee. They are made by steeping them in salted water for a few weeks. Boiled, their whites turn opaque and the yolks a brilliant orange.

Century eggs are made differently, coated with a paste made of mud and rice husks and kept in a dark place for weeks until their whites turn black and their yolks a dull grey. The name century eggs suggests that they are preserved for 100 years. This is a complete myth.

Fertilized duck or hen's eggs that contain the chicken or duck embryo called balut are very much an acquired taste.

*Left: Chicken is usually divided into equal portions on the bone, rather than filleted, before it is cooked in stews or curries. The skin is often left on to keep the meat moist.*

# MEAT

The consumption of meat varies from region to region, often depending on the dominant faith. In general, meats eaten tend to be related to the restrictions of Islam, Hinduism and Buddhism. Among the Christians and Taoists (ancestor worshippers) there are fewer taboos. Muslims eschew pork, Hindus and devout Buddhists do not eat beef. Beef and mutton therefore are the favourite Indonesian meats.

In Indonesia, most of the people are Muslims, but Hinduism is practised by as many as 93 per cent of the people of Bali, and found in parts of Sumatra, Java, Lombok and Kalimantan. Officially, only 3 per cent of Indonesians are Hindus, but Indonesian beliefs are too complex to classify as belonging to a single religion. In Java, a substantial number of Muslims follow a non-orthodox, Hindu-influenced form of Islam known as 'Islam Abangan' or 'Islam Kejawèn', while across the archipelago the Hindu legacy, along with the other mystic traditions, influences popular beliefs and cuisine.

### BEEF

Beef is enjoyed in Indonesia, apart from in Hindu Bali and among Buddhists. Much of the beef eaten in Indonesia comes from water buffalo meat, in long-cooked, dry curries such as rendang, kormas and smoor dishes. Beef satay is popular throughout Indonesia as a staple barbecue item.

*Above, clockwise from top: Beef, lamb shoulder and pork belly.*

*Below: Spare ribs are enjoyed marinated in sticky sauce and barbecued.*

*Below: Pork leg is good roasted and in stews.*

### LAMB AND MUTTON

Lamb is a high-quality protein food. Unlike pork, which are often forbidden for religious reasons, lamb features in all meat-eating cuisines. Lamb and mutton are not widely available in Indonesia and therefore less popular; invariably goat meat is more easily available and cheaper.

### BUFFALO

In Asia, two main types of water buffalo, the river buffalo and the swamp buffalo, are found in huge numbers. Buffalo meat is similar to beef, with the corresponding cuts that can be roasted, grilled (broiled), pan-fried, stewed or braised. However, buffalo is not usually so tender as beef and benefits from being well marinated.

### PORK

This is a comparatively inexpensive meat and it is also the most versatile with an excellent flavour. Look for firm, pale pink flesh. Balinese chefs have myriad ways to cook pork. Lechon and guleng are classic examples of traditional Balinese festive dishes, whole suckling pigs (guleng or guleng celeng) being the offering. This is an iconic Balinese dish, much revered as a festive item. A whole baby pig (suckling) weighing about 8kg/18lb is marinated in a host of spices and roasted on hot charcoal until a rosy red with crisp crackling skin. It is believed to have originated in Polynesia centuries ago when whole pigs were roasted on hot coals at *al fresco* feasts (*luau*).

Types of pork cuts in Indonesia are quite different from the Western form and lean more towards the Chinese choices. Leg of pork is preferred for stews, and belly for stock and grills, stir-fries and curries.

In non-Muslim Indonesia, pork usually end up in satays and curries. Virtually every part of the pig is eaten and offal is highly popular in sambals and curries.

### Pork products

Minced (ground) pork is used to make meatballs and fillings for other recipes; it is also added to porridge for late-night supper dishes.

In non-Muslim Java, they are made into long sausages called celeng, often spiced and fried or steamed. They look much like Western sausages. Pork skin ends up fried as lard chips for garnish.

# HERBS AND SPICES

Integral to all Asian cooking, ground up in complex blends or used as top notes in curries, soups and stir-fries, herbs and spices play fundamental roles in Indonesian cooking. Within the plethora of dried whole spices, powders and fresh herbs, the permutations are endless. Subtle, pungent or heady fresh herbs such as basil, lemon grass, coriander (cilantro), mint, chillies, lime leaves, ginger and other esoterics are reputed to have medicinal and restorative properties.

Dried spice powders such as coriander, cumin, fenugreek, aniseed, turmeric and chilli all find a place within the spectrum of spicy cooking. Other flavouring ingredients include tamarind both fresh and dried, in pastes and concentrates, sesame seeds, dried lily buds, sugar cane, palm sugar (jaggery) and limes. The use of herbs in the preparation of curry pastes and sambals is not an exact science. It is learned by experience.

Many of the spices and herbs are grown in every home vegetable plot, market farm, hillside and backyard throughout Indonesia. Indeed, many a dish would be a pale shadow of itself but for a herb or two, chopped, torn or added to curries in the last minute to impart their unique, and often elusive, perfumes.

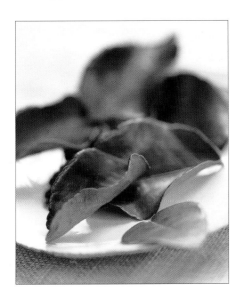

*Above: Kaffir lime leaves have a strong and wonderfully zesty fragrance.*

*Above: The fresh flavour of mint complements many Asian dishes.*

## FRESH HERBS

Essential for giving a wonderful aroma and explosion of flavour to many dishes.

### Laksa leaves

With the botanical name of polygonum, this fragrant leaf has been adopted by Indonesians and is almost *de rigueur* in Indonesian curries, as well as the laksas that gave it its common name. Small, thin leaves jut from slender stalks that have a distinct lemony perfume with hints of coriander, mint and basil. Indeed, a variety grown in Vietnam known as rau rum is also called Vietnamese coriander or mint.

### Lime leaves

Also known as kaffir lime leaves, these are native to the Indonesian culinary heritage. Grown widely in all tropical regions, the plant is used mainly for its leaves, which have a distinctive citrus perfume when crushed. Each leaf is shaped like a guitar or figure eight. The fruit is walnut-sized, with a gnarled, bright green skin.

### Mint

The most commonly used mint in Indonesia is similar to the garden peppermint of the West. It is furry-leaved with a sweet flavour. It is used in salads and as a garnish, often in combination with basil and coriander. There are numerous varieties of mint, including spearmint and peppermint,

*Above: Holy basil has a distinct and delicious flavour. It is well worth cultivating a plant on your windowsill.*

differing widely in size, shape and flavour. The mint leaves sold in supermarkets work well as a substitute.

### Pandan leaf

Popular in Indonesia, screwpine, commonly known as pandan leaf, grows like a weed in tropical climes. Used as much for its green colouring as for its perfume, pandan leaf imparts a distinctive, vanilla-like scent to puddings. It is also used as a natural wrapper for deep-frying. The long, narrow leaves are knotted or bruised to release their unique flavour before use. The leaves are available fresh or dried in some Asian markets. Some stores also stock pandan extract, but if you can't find either, you could use vanilla pods (beans) instead.

### Holy basil

The basil family is large and diverse, encompassing different shapes, sizes, colours and aromatic nuances. The most common varieties found in Asia are Thai sweet basil, holy basil and lemon basil. Thai sweet has the broadest range: aromatically similar to anise, it is mild enough to be eaten as a salad vegetable. In Indonesian cooking, basil is almost always used raw, sprinkled on noodle soups, tossed in salads or added to curries. Asian basil is found in Asian markets, but the sweet Mediterranean basil found in all supermarkets can be substituted.

*Above: Chinese chives have a good flavour and make a pretty garnish.*

## Chives

Across Asia, chives are found in three forms: green chives, with flat stems and slim-bladed leaves; yellow, the same grown under a cloche, which explains its pallor; and Chinese flowering, whose sturdier round leaves are tipped by pointed pale green buds, like little unopened flowers. All have a mild spring onion (scallion) flavour with a hint of garlic.

## Coriander (cilantro)

Originally from Central Asia, and ubiquitous in most tropical and temperate countries' cuisines, coriander is the most common culinary herb, especially the seeds, which are ground into powder as a key ingredient in curries. The perfumed leaves are used liberally, especially in soups, pancit dishes, dumpling mixes and garnishes. Bunches of fresh leaves are available in many Asian markets.

## Salam leaves (Indonesian bay leaves)

Also known as Indonesian laurel, this herb is not actually a member of the bay family. It can be used fresh or dry and is often added to soups or steamed dishes. Available in Asian stores.

## Curry leaves

Very much an Indian herb, curry leaves have diamond-shaped leaves that are tough, bottle-green and hang in even rows from thin stems. They have a warm, peppery scent with citrus notes when crushed. They add a distinct flavour to seafood curries, chutneys, rasams (sour soups) and relishes.

## CHILLIES

Both fresh and dried chillies are used with abandon in Indonesian food. Most pastes would use dried chillies as they have a more intense red colour, while fresh chillies are the norm for delicate seafood curries, salads and as a dip with soy sauce. There are many types of chillies, their fire ranging from barely-there to flaming inferno! Green ones are often eaten raw like a vegetable.

## Thai bird chillies

These tiny pods have a fire that is disproportionate to their size. They come in many colours, ranging from pale yellow to green, orange and bright red, and are best seeded as the seeds are overpoweringly hot. Only two or three Thai bird chillies are sufficient to give incendiary fire to curries and soups. They are available fresh and dried in Asian stores and supermarkets.

## Dried chillies

These are also used to make chilli oil, by infusing them in palm or grape seed oil. Dried chillies can be bought whole, or chopped, in Asian stores and some supermarkets. For complex curry pastes, they are preferred to fresh chilli. If kept in a dry, cool place, dried chillies have a long shelf life.

## Chilli powder

This fiery, deep-red powder is made by finely grinding dried red chillies. Any chilli can be used but the hottest powder is made from the dried Thai bird chillies.

## Chilli paste

This is made by grinding red chillies, seeded or otherwise, into a fine paste. Whether you add ground garlic, ginger or aromatics depends on what the paste

### Preparing dried chillies

**1** Remove the stems and seeds with a knife. Cut into pieces and place in a bowl.

**2** Pour over hot water and leave to soak for about 30 minutes. Drain and use according to the recipe.

*Left: Green chillies may be fiery hot but are often munched as a vegetable.*

*Above: Cardamom seeds add a highly distinctive scent to curries.*

*Above: Bundles of cinnamon can be bought cheaply in Asian markets.*

*Above: Cloves add warm flavour to many curries, stews and desserts.*

is going to be used for. Oil is added if you want a smooth consistency. Versatile and popular, it is used to season sauces, added to curry pastes, or as a condiment to salads, relishes and dips for fried snacks. Ready-made chilli paste is sold in jars in Asian markets.

## DRY SPICES AND HERBS

These store-cupboard staples give the essential warmth and depth of flavour.

### Agar agar

Not strictly a spice or herb, agar agar, known by the same generic name in Indonesia and plays an important role in Indonesian kitchens. Similar to gelatine, agar agar is a gum that is extracted from dried seaweed and processed into white translucent sticks, or ground to a powder. Once dissolved in boiling water, it turns to jelly and is widely used in jellied desserts. Agar agar is available in stick or powder form in Asian stores.

### Cardamom

Grown widely in the Middle East, India and Nepal, cardamoms come in two varieties – large black and small green pods. They play an important role as a peppery note in rice dishes, soups and curries. Black cardamoms are used sparingly as they are hard to come by. Green cardamoms are added whole to a range of curries but must be discarded before serving as they are not edible as such, only used for their spicy aroma.

### Cinnamon

A member of the cassia family, the cinnamon tree is grown widely in the Himalayas, Sri Lanka, China and South-east Asia. The most common type is the bark of the Chinese cinnamon, which is thick, rich in oils and a deep brown colour. A pungent ingredient with constituents of volatile oil, cinnamon is added to soups and rice dishes and some cakes. It is widely available.

### Cloves

This spice has been known worldwide since the 5th century and is produced on a large scale in Indonesia. It is used primarily as a culinary herb in soups, cakes and stews. It has a distinctive liquorice flavour and is available in most Indian stores and supermarkets.

### Sesame seeds

These tiny white or black seeds are commonly used in many Indonesian dishes. They have a subtle nutty flavour and are often used to coat meats for deep-frying, or are sprinkled on stir-fries. Ground up and cooked with sugar as a thick gruel, sesame seeds are a favourite snack.

### Star anise

Also known as Chinese anise, this is the dried, star-shaped fruit of a slender evergreen tree that grows in China, India and Japan, where the bark is ground to powder and burnt as incense in temples. Not related to aniseed, star anise imparts a strong liquorice flavour and is often used with cloves in aromatic soups and curries. Whole, or crushed, star anise is one of the principal ingredients in five-spice powder. The whole spice is a dried eight-pointed star, the fruit of an evergreen tree native to south-west China. Star anise tastes and smells like anised. The ground spice goes will with duck, while the whole spice can be used in slow-cooked dishes. It is available from Asian stores and most supermarkets, sold whole or as a powder.

*Left: Star anise imparts good flavour to savoury dishes and looks attractive, but is too tough and woody to be eaten. It makes a pretty addition to fruit dishes.*

## AROMATICS AND ROOT HERBS

These are the base ingredients of many spice pastes, marinades and sauces.

### Garlic

Highly prized for more than 5000 years, garlic is a member of the onion genus. Each bulb can contain up to 10 cloves, which should be firm with a pungent aroma and flavour. Chopped or crushed, garlic is fried in oil to impart flavour to stir-fries, curries, stews and noodles. It is also used raw to flavour pickles, dips, marinades and sauces. Garlic is thought to be good for the heart. It is available in Asian stores and all supermarkets.

### Galangal

Although a member of the ginger family and similar in appearance, galangal is never eaten raw. Its aroma and flavour are best used in tandem with shallots, garlic and chillies in spice pastes and in marinades. The roots can be sliced or bruised and added to soups and curries to impart a more subtle flavour. When young, the rhizomes are creamy pink in colour and have a lemony flavour; the more mature roots are golden and peppery. Fresh galangal will keep for about one week if sealed in a plastic bag and refrigerated. It can also be frozen. Both dried and bottled galangal purée (paste) are available from Asian stores.

### Lesser galangal

These little fingers of dark brown ginger are an important herb in Indonesia, often replacing ordinary ginger and

*Above: Shallots give a sweet and subtle flavour to wet spice blends.*

galangal in spice mixes. Lesser galangal has a faint anise flavour and a strong after taste, and is best used fairly cautiously for this reason.

### Ginger

Indigenous to most of South-east Asia, ginger is the oldest and most widely used flavouring across the Asian region, especially in Indian and Indonesian cooking. A herbaceous perennial plant, ginger is knobbly-looking with a smooth, beige skin, and is sold as two types. Young, pale yellow ginger is fresh-looking and tender with a slightly sweet pungency and can be chopped or shredded for stir-fries, stews, rice,

pickles, steamed dishes and puddings. Older ginger is more fibrous and is usually ground into spice blends or pickled as a relish.

Well-documented in traditional Chinese medicine and Indian Ayurvedic practice for its carminative and expectorant action, ginger is believed to be good for alleviating motion sickness and bronchial problems. Fresh ginger is readily available in Asian stores and supermarkets. Choose smooth, plump roots and store in a cool, dry place.

### Lemon grass

A woody, fibrous stalk, lemon grass is used throughout all South-east Asian culinary cultures. It imparts a fragrant, citrus flavour to dishes. The pale yellowish-green, paper-like sheath that encases it has to be removed before use. The root end is chopped, pounded or crushed before being added to spice blends, stir-fries, curries and marinades. Lemon grass is one of the principal ingredients in Indonesian cooking. It is available fresh and dried in Asian stores and some supermarkets.

### Shallots

These small, marble-sized bulbs form the basis of many spice blends and when deep-fried in oil make a crunchy garnish in many Indonesian soups and stews. Green onions, the stems of shallots, appear in many dishes and are often chopped and used as a garnish, added to lumpia and other snacks and stir-fries at the last minute.

*Above: Fat bulbs of garlic are a kitchen essential for most cuisines.*

*Above: Galangal is similar to ginger but has a more specifically 'Asian' flavour.*

*Above: A piece of fresh root ginger gives heat and flavour to many dishes.*

Green onions and spring onions (scallions), which do not mature into shallots, are often confused and have the same culinary uses.

## Turmeric

Fresh turmeric root has a subtle, earthy taste and imparts a vivid colour and flavour to spice blends. It may also be dried and ground to a deep-yellow powder that imparts good colour and only a slight hint of flavour. Both fresh and dried are found in Asian markets.

## OTHER STORE CUPBOARD ESSENTIALS

These ingredients are useful to keep in supply for the recipes in this book.

## Bean sauces

Condiments made from soya beans that have been fermented and puréed come in various guises. Yellow beans are processed into a sauce called taucheo, which is often served on its own or mixed with other ingredients to make a dip. Black beans are made into black bean sauce, a staple in Cantonese cooking. Salty and pungent, bean sauces are used as full-bodied seasonings much like soy sauce, but with more flavour.

## Oyster sauce

This thick, brown sauce is known by its common English name. Made from dried oyster extract, sugar, water and salt, strongly flavoured and salty, it is used as a complete seasoning, obviating the need for salt in stir-fries. It is an import into Indonesia, being a resoundingly Cantonese product. It makes a good seasoning for soups and stews and is widely available in Asian stores and good supermarkets.

## Palm sugar (jaggery)

Widely used in South-east Asia, palm sugar is extracted from the sap of various palm trees, mostly the coconut. There are several types used in Indonesian cooking. One is dark brown and comes in little can-shaped cylinders, and another is in the form of round cakes of a pale peach colour. There is also a thick liquid version in cans that is easier to use. Solid palm sugar has to be scraped, shredded or melted before use. Indian grocers sell

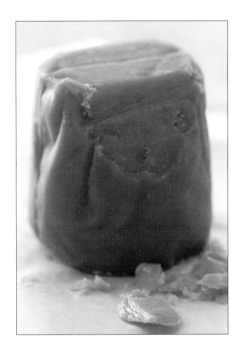

*Above: A block of palm sugar, which can be shaved or melted as required.*

another type called jaggery that is basically similar but comes in rough nuggets or cakes. It is indispensable in Indonesian desserts and puddings. Available in Indian, Malaysian and Thai stores.

## Sesame oil

Extracted from the seeds, sesame oil is commonly used in stir-fried dishes. Two types are available: plain, pale golden oil, which is mildly nutty and good for frying; and the darker, richer tasting oil made from roasted sesame seeds and usually added in small quantities as a top note just before serving.

## Soy sauce

Probably the most commonly used sauce throughout Asia is soy sauce in its various guises. Made from fermented soya beans, wheat and yeast, soy sauce may be light, dark or with mushroom flavouring. Dark soy is used as a marinade for its mahogany colour as well as its saltiness. Light soy sauce is used like salt and has a tantalizing flavour when mixed with lime juice and chillies as a dip. Naturally fermented soy sauce will not keep forever, but does have a fairly long shelf-life.

Indonesia produces kecap manis, which is a thick black soy sauce with a powerful aroma and a very sweet syrupy taste, and kecap asin which is much thinner and weaker and is sometimes described as white soy. Kecap sedang comes somewhere in between but is less popular than kecap manis.

## Tamarind

A legume tree grown widely in tropical savannas in Africa, India and Malaysia, tamarind bears brittle long brown pods. Each pod may contain 5–10 seeds joined by tough fibres in a mass of sweetish, acid brown pulp. It is this that features widely in Indonesian curries. Tamarind comes in various forms: blocks of paste with seeds in it; a dried pod; or processed as a thick concentrate. The fresh pods and dried pulp are available from Asian stores. Easier to find and use are the tubs of tamarind concentrate, which is simply diluted in water to give a sour fruitiness to dishes. Tamarind is available in most Asian markets.

---

### Preparing tamarind from paste

Many recipes from Indonesia and other areas of South-east Asia will call for tamarind, so it is worth obtaining a tamarind block and having it as a store-cupboard staple. You will need warm water and a nylon sieve (strainer) to prepare it.

**1** Crumble 300g/11oz of the block and mix with 500ml/17fl oz/ 2 generous cups water. Strain through a fine sieve to obtain a sour, dark brown liquid. Store in a screw-top jar.

**2** Add as much tamarind solution as taste dictates to fish and shellfish curries, using a clean spoon to scoop it out each time to avoid contamination.

# SOUPS, STEWS AND SNACKS

In the hustle and bustle of urban life, Indonesians rely

on street snacks for much of their daily sustenance.

Hot and fragrant broths filled with meat, seafood and

vegetables and succulent street snacks are popular.

Satay — a spicy skewer of grilled meat or fish — is the

best-known snack, which is often eaten with a chilli dip.

# UNRIPE PAPAYA SOUP

*THIS IS A LIGHTLY-SPICED AND HERBY SOUP FROM INDONESIA THAT MAKES GOOD USE OF UNRIPE PAPAYA AND IS AN IDEAL START TO ANY MEAL. IT IS THE KIND OF SOUP MEANT TO PREPARE THE TASTEBUDS FOR WHAT IS YET TO COME — LIGHT AND REFRESHING TO THE PALATE.*

### SERVES FOUR

INGREDIENTS

   1 unripe papaya, about 800g/1¾lb
   45ml/3 tbsp vegetable oil
   1 litre/1¾ pints/4 cups water
   4 salam leaves (Indonesian bay
     leaves) or sweet basil leaves
   2 lemon grass stalks, 5cm/2in of root
     end bruised
   2.5ml/½ tsp ground black pepper
   5ml/1 tsp salt
   fried shallots or serundeng, to garnish
For the spice paste
   2 lemon grass stalks, 5cm/2in of root
     end finely chopped
   6 shallots, finely chopped
   5 garlic cloves, finely chopped
   10g/¼oz galangal
   15g/½oz terasi (Indonesian
     shrimp paste)
   2.5ml/½ tsp turmeric powder
   4 fresh red chillies, seeded and
     finely chopped
   5ml/1 tsp coriander seeds
   10g/¼oz lesser galangal

**1** Grind the spice paste ingredients to a textured paste using a mortar and pestle or an electric food processor or blender.

**2** Peel the papaya with a vegetable peeler and slice into two lengthways. Discard any soft pulp and seeds.

**3** Slice the papaya into long strips and then crosswise into pieces about 5mm/¼in thick.

**COOK'S TIP**
It can be difficult to find salam leaves outside of large Asian markets, but fresh bay leaves will work in this recipe and may be used instead.

**4** Heat the oil and fry the spice paste over a low heat for 10 minutes, stirring constantly until the fragrances are released and the oil separates.

**5** Bring the water to the boil and stir in the fried spice paste. Simmer for 3 minutes.

**6** Add the papaya slices, salam leaves, lemon grass, pepper and salt. Cook for 5–8 minutes until the papaya slices are just tender.

**7** While the papaya is cooking, prepare your garnishes of fried sliced shallots or serundeng and warm the soup bowls.

**8** Take the papaya soup off the heat. Adjust the seasoning if necessary and serve it in individual bowls, garnished as you wish.

**Per Portion** Energy 189kcal/791kJ; Protein 5.1g; Carbohydrate 21.8g, of which sugars 18.8g; Fat 9.8g, of which saturates 1.1g; Cholesterol 19mg; Calcium 137mg; Fibre 5.2g; Sodium 181mg.

# PUMPKIN, BEAN AND BAMBOO SOUP WITH COCONUT

*THIS TASTY SOUP IS FROM JAVA, WHERE IT IS SERVED ON ITS OWN WITH RICE OR AS AN ACCOMPANIMENT TO A POACHED OR GRILLED FISH DISH. IN SOME PARTS OF JAVA, THE DISH INCLUDES SMALL PRAWNS (SHRIMP) BUT, IF IT IS PACKED WITH VEGETABLES ALONE, IT MAKES AN EXTREMELY SATISFYING VEGETARIAN MEAL. GENERALLY, THIS SOUP IS ACCOMPANIED BY A CHILLI SAMBAL, WHICH CAN BE MADE BY POUNDING CHILLIES WITH SHRIMP PASTE AND LIME JUICE, OR WITH GINGER AND GARLIC.*

SERVES FOUR TO SIX

INGREDIENTS
- 30ml/2 tbsp palm, groundnut (peanut) or corn oil
- 150g/5oz pumpkin flesh
- 115g/4oz yard-long beans, cut in pieces
- 220g/7¾oz can bamboo shoots, drained and rinsed
- 900ml/1½ pints/3¾ cups coconut milk
- 10ml/2 tsp palm sugar (jaggery)
- 130g/4½oz fresh coconut, grated
- salt

For the spice paste
- 4 shallots, chopped
- 25g/1oz fresh root ginger, chopped
- 4 fresh red chillies, seeded and chopped
- 2 garlic cloves, chopped
- 5ml/1 tsp coriander seeds
- 4 candlenuts, toasted and chopped

To serve
- cooked rice
- chilli sambal

**1** Grind the spice paste ingredients to a textured paste using a mortar and pestle or an electric food processor or blender.

**2** Heat the oil in a wok or large, heavy pan, stir in the spice paste and fry until fragrant. Toss the pumpkin, yard-long beans and bamboo shoots in the paste and pour in the coconut milk. Add the sugar and bring to the boil.

**3** Reduce the heat and cook gently for 5–10 minutes, until the vegetables are just tender.

**4** Season the soup with salt to taste and stir in half the fresh coconut. Place the cooked rice in individual warmed bowls, then ladle the soup over the top, sprinkle with the remaining coconut and serve with a chilli sambal.

**COOK'S TIPS**
- Bamboo shoots are available in cans in most Chinese and South-east Asian markets and stores, as well as being sold in large supermarkets.
- If yard-long beans are unavailable, use French (green) beans in their place.

**VARIATION**
When pumpkins are not in season, use a different member of the squash family, such as butternut squash or acorn squash, for a change of flavour.

**Per Portion** Energy 333kcal/1388kJ; Protein 6g; Carbohydrate 26g, of which sugars 23.8g; Fat 23.6g, of which saturates 11.7g; Cholesterol 0mg; Calcium 115mg; Fibre 4.9g; Sodium 258mg.

# CORN, TAPIOCA AND PUMPKIN SOUP WITH FRESH BASIL LEAVES

*IN RURAL AREAS OF SULAWESI, WHERE FARMING IS THE MAIN INDUSTRY, THE WORKING DAY BEGINS AT THE CRACK OF DAWN. THIS IS AN EASY-TO-COOK DISH FROM THE REGION THAT IS BOTH NOURISHING AND DELICIOUS BECAUSE OF THE TAPIOCA AND PUMPKIN. IT IS A SOUP THAT CAN BE PREPARED THE NIGHT BEFORE AND QUICKLY WARMED UP FOR A CONVENIENT AND SATISFYING SNACK.*

**1** Steam the tapioca and pumpkin for 15 minutes until soft. Meanwhile, bring the water to the boil, add the rice and cook for 10 minutes.

**2** Cut the tapioca into smaller chunks and add to the rice and water with the pumpkin, lemon grass and corn. Cook for 10 minutes, stirring until all the ingredients form a thick consistency.

**3** Add the basil leaves, spinach and salt and pepper. Taste and adjust the seasoning if necessary. Serve the soup piping hot.

## SERVES FOUR TO SIX

### INGREDIENTS

115g/4oz tapioca flesh, chopped
115g/4oz pumpkin or butternut
  squash flesh, chopped
800ml/28fl oz/3¼ cups water
30ml/2 tbsp rice
2 lemon grass stalks, 5cm/2in of root
  end bruised
60ml/4 tbsp corn kernels
10 sweet basil leaves
75g/3oz spinach
5ml/1 tsp salt
2.5ml/½ tsp ground
  black pepper

### COOK'S TIPS

• Tapioca is sold at many Asian, Chinese and Caribbean stores. It has a dark brown skin and pale white flesh. Use frozen or processed tapioca for this soup if the fresh version is unavailable.
• After step 2, you can chill or freeze the soup for another time. Just add the final ingredients at serving time.

**Per Portion** Energy 89kcal/379kJ; Protein 0.6g; Carbohydrate 22.6g, of which sugars 0.3g; Fat 0.1g, of which saturates 0g; Cholesterol 0mg; Calcium 8mg; Fibre 0.3g; Sodium 1mg.

# SPICY AUBERGINE SOUP
## WITH BEEF AND LIME

*A DELICIOUS SOUPY STEW FROM NORTH SUMATRA, THIS DISH CAN BE MADE WITH AUBERGINES, GREEN JACKFRUIT OR ANY OF THE SQUASH FAMILY. FOR AN AUTHENTIC MEAL, SERVE THE SOUP WITH A BOWL OF RICE AND A CHILLI SAMBAL, BEARING IN MIND THAT THE QUANTITY OF RICE SHOULD BE GREATER THAN THE SOUPY STEW, AS THE ROLE OF THE SOUP IS TO MOISTEN AND FLAVOUR THE RICE.*

### SERVES FOUR

INGREDIENTS
  30ml/2 tbsp palm, groundnut
    (peanut) or corn oil
  150g/5oz lean beef, cut into
    thin strips
  500ml/17fl oz/2 cups
    coconut milk
  10ml/2 tsp sugar
  3–4 Thai aubergines (eggplants) or
    1 large Mediterranean aubergine,
    cut into wedges
  3–4 kaffir lime leaves
  juice of 1 lime
  salt
For the spice paste
  4 shallots, chopped
  4 fresh red Thai chillies, seeded
    and chopped
  25g/1oz fresh root
    ginger, chopped
  15g/½oz fresh turmeric, chopped,
    or 2.5ml/½ tsp ground turmeric
  2 garlic cloves, chopped
  5ml/1 tsp coriander seeds
  2.5ml/½ tsp cumin seeds
  2–3 candlenuts
To serve
  cooked rice
  1 lime, quartered (optional)
  chilli sambal (optional)

**1** Grind the spice paste ingredients to a coarse paste using a mortar and pestle or an electric food processor or blender.

**2** Heat the oil in a wok or heavy pan, stir in the spice paste and fry until fragrant. Add the beef, stirring to coat it well in the spice paste, then add the coconut milk and sugar. Bring the liquid to the boil, then reduce the heat and simmer gently for 10 minutes.

**3** Add the aubergine wedges and kaffir lime leaves to the pan and cook gently for a further 5–10 minutes, until tender but not mushy. Stir in the lime juice and season with salt to taste.

**4** Ladle the soup into individual warmed bowls and serve with bowls of cooked rice to spoon the soup over, wedges of lime to squeeze on the top and a chilli sambal to eat alongside, if you like.

Per Portion Energy 224kcal/938kJ; Protein 12.1g; Carbohydrate 14.6g, of which sugars 12.6g; Fat 13.6g, of which saturates 3.2g; Cholesterol 22mg; Calcium 79mg; Fibre 3g; Sodium 181mg.

# SPICY TRIPE SOUP WITH LEMON GRASS AND LIME

*THIS POPULAR INDONESIAN SOUP IS PACKED WITH SPICES AND THE REFRESHING FLAVOURS OF LEMON GRASS AND LIME. STEAMING BOWLS OF SOTO BABAT ARE SOUGHT AFTER AT FOOD STALLS AS A GREAT PICK-ME-UP. THE LOCALS PREFER THEIR TRIPE TO BE CHEWY FOR THIS SPICY SOUP, WHICH IS SERVED WITH A PUNGENT CHILLI SAMBAL, BUT IF YOU PREFER, YOU CAN COOK IT FOR LONGER SO THAT THE TRIPE IS TENDER.*

### SERVES FOUR

INGREDIENTS
- 250ml/8fl oz/1 cup rice wine vinegar
- 900g/2lb beef tripe, cleaned
- 2 litres/3½ pints/8 cups beef stock or water
- 2–3 garlic cloves, crushed
- 2 lemon grass stalks, lightly crushed with a mallet or rolling pin
- 25g/1oz fresh root ginger, grated
- 3–4 kaffir lime leaves
- 225g/8oz mooli (daikon) or turnip, finely sliced
- 15ml/1 tbsp palm, groundnut (peanut) or vegetable oil
- 4 shallots, finely sliced
- salt and ground black pepper

For the sambal
- 15ml/1 tbsp palm, groundnut (peanut) or vegetable oil
- 2 garlic cloves, crushed
- 2–3 fresh hot red chillies, seeded and finely chopped
- 15ml/1 tbsp Chilli and Shrimp Paste (see page 19)
- 2.5ml/5 tsp tomato purée (paste)

**1** Fill a large pan with about 2.5 litres/ 4½ pints/11¼ cups water and bring it to the boil. Reduce the heat and stir in the vinegar. Add the tripe, season with salt and pepper and simmer on a low heat for about 1 hour.

**2** Meanwhile, prepare the sambal. Heat the oil in a small, heavy pan. Stir in the garlic and chillies and fry until fragrant. Stir in the chilli and shrimp paste, then add the tomato purée and mix until thoroughly combined. Transfer the paste to a small dish and put aside.

**3** When the tripe is cooked, drain and cut into bitesize squares or strips. Pour the stock or water into a large pan and bring it to the boil. Reduce the heat and add the tripe, garlic, lemon grass, ginger, lime leaves and mooli or turnip.

**4** Cook gently for 15–20 minutes, until the mooli or turnip is tender. (For tender tripe, omit the mooli or turnip at this stage, simmer the tripe for 4–5 hours and then add the mooli or turnip for the last 15 minutes of cooking.)

**5** Meanwhile, heat the oil in a small frying pan. Add the shallots and fry for about 5 minutes until golden brown. Drain on kitchen paper.

**6** Ladle the soup into individual warmed bowls and sprinkle the shallots over the top. Serve the soup with the spicy sambal, which can be added in a spoonful and stirred in or served in a bowl on the side, according to individual taste.

**Per Portion** Energy 160kcal/668kJ; Protein 19.2g; Carbohydrate 5.5g, of which sugars 4.8g; Fat 7g, of which saturates 1.1g; Cholesterol 163mg; Calcium 198mg; Fibre 1.9g; Sodium 299mg.

# CORN AND CRAB SOUP

*THIS DISH IS BELIEVED TO HAVE ORIGINATED IN JAVA, WHERE AT SOME TIME IT WAS COPIED FROM THE CHINESE IMMIGRANTS. IT IS NOW A WELL-LOVED SOUP THROUGHOUT THE ISLANDS, EATEN WHENEVER CORN AND CRAB ARE PLENTIFUL. IT MAKES A DELICIOUS APPETIZER, OR A LIGHT LUNCH WITH RICE OR BREAD.*

SERVES FOUR

INGREDIENTS
750ml/1¼ pints/3 cups water
1 seafood stock cube
450g/1lb can creamed corn
5ml/1 tsp salt
15ml/1 tbsp sesame oil
250g/9oz crab meat
2 eggs
2 spring onions (scallions),
 trimmed and sliced, to garnish
black vinegar, to serve

**2** Simmer for 5 minutes, then add the crab meat and cook for 3 minutes.

**1** Combine all the ingredients except for the crab meat and eggs in a pan and bring to the boil.

**3** Lightly beat the eggs and add to the barely simmering soup, stirring quickly to distribute the egg evenly and thicken the soup.

**4** Adjust the seasoning and serve garnished with spring onions, with a dish of black vinegar on the side.

**COOK'S TIPS**
• Nothing quite matches the flavour of fresh crab, but Scandinavian canned crab is an acceptable substitute when the fresh variety is not available.
• Use regular corn and add a dash of cream or coconut cream if you cannot obtain creamed corn.
• Black vinegar is made from fermented rice, millet, wheat, sorghum and barley. Its flavour varies from region to region.

**Per Portion** Energy 279kcal/1173kJ; Protein 18.6g; Carbohydrate 29.9g, of which sugars 10.8g; Fat 10.3g, of which saturates 1.9g; Cholesterol 140mg; Calcium 19mg; Fibre 1.6g; Sodium 1093mg.

# INDONESIAN CHICKEN BROTH

*THIS IS PERHAPS THE MOST POPULAR OF ALL INDONESIAN SOUPS. THROUGHOUT SOUTH-EAST ASIA YOU WILL FIND VARIATIONS OF THIS SOUP; EVEN IN INDONESIA IT VARIES FROM REGION TO REGION, SUCH AS THE BALI VERSION THAT INCLUDES NOODLES INSTEAD OF POTATOES.*

**2** Heat the oil in a heavy pan, stir in the ginger, turmeric, lemon grass, kaffir lime leaves, candlenuts, garlic, coriander seeds and terasi and fry until the mixture begins to darken and become fragrant. Pour in the chicken stock, bring to the boil, then reduce the heat and simmer for about 20 minutes.

**3** Meanwhile, heat the oil for deep-frying in a wok. Add the potato slices and fry until crisp and golden brown. Remove from the pan with a slotted spoon, drain on kitchen paper and put aside.

**4** Strain the flavoured chicken stock and reserve. Pour back into the pan and season with salt and pepper to taste. Return to the boil, then reduce the heat and add the chicken. Simmer for 2–3 minutes until cooked but still tender.

## SERVES FOUR TO SIX

INGREDIENTS
- 30ml/2 tbsp palm, groundnut (peanut) or corn oil
- 25g/1oz fresh root ginger, finely chopped
- 25g/1oz fresh turmeric, finely chopped, or 5ml/1 tsp ground turmeric
- 1 lemon grass stalk, finely chopped
- 4–5 kaffir lime leaves, crushed with fingers
- 4 candlenuts, coarsely crushed
- 2 garlic cloves, crushed
- 5ml/1 tsp coriander seeds
- 5ml/1 tsp terasi (Indonesian shrimp paste)
- 2 litres/3½ pints/8 cups chicken stock
- corn or vegetable oil, for deep-frying
- 2 waxy potatoes, finely sliced
- 350g/12oz skinless chicken breast fillets, thinly sliced widthways
- 150g/5oz leafy green cabbage, finely sliced
- 150g/5oz mung beansprouts
- 3 hard-boiled eggs, thinly sliced
- salt and ground black pepper
- To serve
- 1 bunch fresh coriander (cilantro) leaves, roughly chopped
- 2–3 spring onions (scallions), finely sliced
- 2–3 fresh hot red or green chillies, seeded and finely sliced diagonally
- 2 limes, cut into wedges
- kecap manis (Indonesian sweet soy sauce)

**1** Prepare the serving ingredients by putting the coriander, spring onions, chillies and lime wedges into each serving bowl.

**5** Sprinkle some of the cabbage and beansprouts into the base of each soup bowl. Ladle the broth over the cabbage and beansprouts and divide the chicken between the bowls. Place the boiled eggs and potatoes on top. Serve the hot broth with the serving ingredients.

**Per Portion** Energy 296kcal/1238kJ; Protein 21.1g; Carbohydrate 14.8g, of which sugars 3g; Fat 17.5g, of which saturates 2.8g; Cholesterol 136mg; Calcium 63mg; Fibre 2.7g; Sodium 96mg.

# CRISPY FRIED TEMPEH

*OFTEN COOKED AT STREET STALLS, CRISPY FRIED TEMPEH CAN BE SERVED AS A SNACK OR AS PART OF A SELECTION OF INDONESIAN DISHES. THIS FERMENTED TOFU IS OFTEN SERVED AS A SNACK WITH STIR-FRIED NOODLES OR PLAIN RICE AND PICKLED VEGETABLES.*

### SERVES THREE TO FOUR

### INGREDIENTS

45ml/3 tbsp coconut
  or groundnut (peanut) oil
500g/1¼lb tempeh, cut into
  bitesize strips
4 shallots, finely chopped
4 garlic cloves, finely chopped
25g/1oz fresh galangal or
  fresh root ginger, finely chopped
3–4 fresh red chillies, seeded and
  finely chopped
150ml/¼ pint/⅔ cup kecap manis
  (Indonesian sweet soy sauce)
30ml/2 tbsp unsalted
  peanuts, crushed
1 small bunch fresh coriander
  (cilantro) leaves, roughly chopped
stir-fried noodles or cooked rice,
  to serve

**1** Heat 30ml/2 tbsp of the oil in a wok or large, heavy frying pan. Add the tempeh and stir-fry until golden brown.

**2** Using a slotted spoon, transfer the fried tempeh pieces to crumpled kitchen paper to drain.

**3** Wipe the wok or frying pan clean with kitchen paper.

**4** Heat the remaining 15ml/1 tbsp oil in the wok or pan, stir in the shallots, garlic, galangal and chillies and fry until fragrant and beginning to colour.

**5** Stir in the kecap manis and toss in the fried tempeh. Stir-fry until the sauce has reduced and clings to the tempeh.

**6** Transfer the tempeh to a serving dish and sprinkle with the peanuts and coriander leaves. Serve hot with stir-fried noodles or cooked rice.

**COOK'S TIP**
Tempeh (fermented tofu) can be bought from Chinese and South-east Asian supermarkets. If you are unable to buy it, firm tofu can be used as an alternative.

**Per Portion** Energy 258kcal/1071kJ; Protein 14.8g; Carbohydrate 7.7g, of which sugars 5.5g; Fat 18.9g, of which saturates 2.6g; Cholesterol 0mg; Calcium 682mg; Fibre 1.7g; Sodium 2680mg.

# BOILED AND FRIED EGGS WITH HOT SAMBAL

*THE TWO-STEP METHOD EMPLOYED HERE RESULTS IN THE MOST MOUTHWATERING DISH. WARUNGS (STREET STALLS) SELL THE EGGS AS AN ACCOMPANIMENT TO OTHER DISHES OR SIMPLY AS A SNACK. WHEN YOU ARE MAKING THE SAMBAL, CONSIDER DOING A LARGE BATCH, AS IT IS A MASTER SAUCE THAT GOES WITH MANY SALADS, STIR-FRIES AND GRILLED FOODS.*

SERVES FOUR

INGREDIENTS
  4 hard-boiled eggs, shelled
  15ml/1 tbsp vegetable oil
  sliced cucumber, to serve (optional)
For the sambal
  2 large onions, finely chopped
  6 garlic cloves, finely chopped
  45g/3 tbsp terasi (Indonesian
    shrimp paste)
  10 dried chillies, soaked in warm
    water until soft, then
    finely chopped
  6 candlenuts
  30g/2 tbsp tomato purée (paste)
  1.5ml/¼ tsp salt
  5ml/1 tsp sugar
  30ml/2 tbsp tamarind concentrate
  45ml/3 tbsp vegetable oil

**2** Fry the mixture in the oil over a low heat until it is fragrant and separates, so that the oil seeps out.

**3** In a clean wok, heat 1 tbsp of oil and fry the eggs all over until a crisp, brown skin forms. Remove the eggs and halve.

**4** To serve, spoon the sambal over the halved eggs, with sliced cucumber on the side, if you like.

**1** Grind the onions, garlic, terasi, chillies and candlenuts using a mortar and pestle until very fine. Add the remaining sambal ingredients, except for the oil, and continue to pound until a rough paste is formed.

**COOK'S TIPS**
• If you omit the frying step for the eggs, you still get a lovely spicy egg dish.
• If you cannot find candlenuts, use about eight macadamia nuts instead.

**Per Portion** Energy 230kcal/956kJ; Protein 14.4g; Carbohydrate 12g, of which sugars 9.1g; Fat 14.3g, of which saturates 2.6g; Cholesterol 247mg; Calcium 198mg; Fibre 2g; Sodium 1070mg.

# SPICY CORN PATTIES

*When it comes to snack food, fried patties and fritters are as popular as grilled fish and satay at the street stalls in Indonesia. Easy to eat with fingers, these corn patties are often served on a square of banana leaf with fresh lime wedges. A small dollop of chilli sambal on the side gives an extra fiery kick to these already fairly spicy snacks.*

SERVES FOUR

INGREDIENTS
2 corn on the cob
15ml/1 tbsp coconut oil
3 eggs
45ml/3 tbsp grated fresh coconut or desiccated (dry unsweetened shredded) coconut
2–3 spring onions (scallions), white parts only, finely sliced
corn or groundnut (peanut) oil, for shallow frying
1 small bunch fresh coriander (cilantro) leaves, roughly chopped
salt and ground black pepper
shredded red chilli, to serve

For the spice paste
3 shallots, finely chopped
2 garlic cloves, finely chopped
25g/1oz fresh galangal or fresh root ginger, finely chopped
1–2 fresh chillies, seeded and finely chopped
2–3 candlenuts, crushed
5ml/1 tsp ground coriander
5ml/1 tsp ground cumin

To serve
1 lime, quartered
chilli sambal or sweet chilli sauce

**2** For the spice paste, grind the shallots, garlic, galangal and chillies to a paste using a mortar and pestle or an electric food processor or blender. Add the candlenuts, coriander and cumin and beat well together.

**3** Heat the coconut oil in a small wok or heavy pan, stir in the spice paste and stir-fry until the paste becomes fragrant and begins to colour. Transfer the paste to a plate and leave to cool.

**4** Beat the eggs in a large bowl. Add the coconut and spring onions and beat in the corn and the cooled spice paste until all the ingredients are thoroughly combined. Season the mixture with salt and pepper.

**5** Heat a thin layer of corn oil or groundnut oil in a heavy frying pan. Working in batches, drop spoonfuls of the corn mixture into the oil and fry the patties for 2–3 minutes on each side, until they are golden brown all over.

**6** Drain the patties on kitchen paper, then arrange them on a serving dish on top of the coriander leaves and garnish with the shreds of red chilli.

**7** Serve the patties hot or at room temperature, with wedges of freshly cut lime to squeeze over them and a chilli sambal or sweet chilli sauce for dipping.

**1** Put the corn on the cob into a large pan of water, bring to the boil and boil for about 8 minutes, until cooked but still firm. Drain the cobs and refresh under running cold water. Use a sharp knife to scrape all the corn off the cob; set aside.

**Per Portion** Energy 368kcal/1531kJ; Protein 10.8g; Carbohydrate 18.1g, of which sugars 8.2g; Fat 28.7g, of which saturates 9.7g; Cholesterol 143mg; Calcium 68mg; Fibre 4.1g; Sodium 196mg.

# SPICY PRAWN AND SCALLOP SATAY

*ONE OF THE TASTIEST SATAY DISHES, THIS IS SUCCULENT, SPICY AND EXTREMELY MOREISH. THE SPICE PASTE IS VERY FRAGRANT, WITH ITS COMBINATION OF GALANGAL, TURMERIC AND LEMON GRASS, AND THE FLAVOURS ARE GIVEN TIME TO PENETRATE THE POUNDED FISH BEFORE BEING COOKED. SERVE WITH RICE AND A FRUITY SALAD OR PICKLED VEGETABLES AND LIME.*

SERVES FOUR

INGREDIENTS
250g/9oz shelled prawns (shrimp), deveined and chopped
250g/9oz shelled scallops, roughly chopped
30ml/2 tbsp potato, tapioca or rice flour
5ml/1 tsp baking powder
12–16 wooden, metal, lemon grass or sugar cane skewers
1 lime, quartered, to serve

For the spice paste
2 shallots, chopped
2 garlic cloves, chopped
2–3 fresh red chillies, seeded and chopped
25g/1oz fresh galangal or fresh root ginger, chopped
15g/½oz fresh turmeric, chopped, or 2.5ml/½ tsp ground turmeric
2–3 lemon grass stalks, chopped
15ml/1 tbsp palm or groundnut (peanut) oil
5ml/1 tsp terasi (Indonesian shrimp paste)
15ml/1 tbsp tamarind paste
5ml/1 tsp palm sugar (jaggery)

**1** To make the spice paste, pound the shallots, garlic, chillies, galangal, turmeric and lemon grass together.

**2** Heat the oil in a wok, stir in the paste and fry until it becomes fragrant and begins to colour. Add the terasi, tamarind and sugar and stir-fry, until the mixture darkens. Leave to cool.

**3** In a bowl, pound the prawns and scallops together to form a paste, or blend them together in an electric blender or food processor.

**4** Beat in the spice paste, followed by the flour and baking powder, until blended. Chill for about 1 hour.

**5** If using wooden skewers, soak in water for about 30 minutes. Prepare the barbecue, or preheat the grill (broiler).

**6** Wrap lumps of the shellfish paste and wrap it around the skewers. Barbecue or grill them for 3 minutes on each side, until golden brown. Serve with the lime wedges to squeeze over.

**Per Portion** Energy 220kcal/922kJ; Protein 27g; Carbohydrate 11.5g, of which sugars 1g; Fat 7.3g, of which saturates 1g; Cholesterol 151mg; Calcium 99mg; Fibre1.5g; Sodium 249mg.

# HOT, SWEET AND SOUR SQUID

*THE INDONESIANS AND MALAYS LOVE COOKING PRAWNS AND SQUID IN THIS WAY, AND EXPERTLY CRUNCH SHELLS AND SUCK TENTACLES TO SAVOUR ALL THE JUICY CHILLI AND TAMARIND FLAVOURING. SWEETENED WITH THE UBIQUITOUS KECAP MANIS, THE ENTICING AROMA OF THESE DELICIOUS SQUID WILL MAKE YOUR TASTEBUDS TINGLE.*

SERVES TWO TO FOUR

INGREDIENTS

   500g/1¼lb fresh baby squid, or
    250g each of fresh baby squid and
    raw king prawns (jumbo shrimp)
   30ml/2 tbsp tamarind paste
   30ml/2 tbsp chilli sauce
   45ml/3 tbsp kecap manis
    (Indonesian sweet soy sauce)
   juice of 1 kalamansi or ordinary lime
   25g/1oz fresh root ginger, grated
   2–4 green chillies, seeded and
    quartered lengthways
   ground black pepper
   fresh coriander (cilantro) leaves and
    lime wedges, to serve

**1** Clean the squid and remove the head and ink sac. Pull out the quill and rinse. Trim the head above the eyes, keeping the tentacles intact. Pat dry the body sac and tentacles and discard the rest.

**2** In a small bowl, mix together the tamarind paste, chilli sauce, kecap manis and lime juice. Beat in the ginger and a little black pepper. Spoon the mixture over the squid and, using your fingers, rub it all over the body sacs and tentacles. Cover and leave to marinate in the refrigerator for 1 hour.

**COOK'S TIP**

To prepare prawns (shrimp) for cooking, devein the prawns and remove the feelers and legs, then rinse, pat dry, and cut along the tail. Marinate and cook in the same way as the squid.

**3** Meanwhile, prepare the barbecue or heat a ridged griddle on the hob. Place the squid on the rack or griddle and cook for 3 minutes on each side, brushing them with the marinade as they cook. Serve immediately with the coriander leaves and lime wedges.

**Per Portion** Energy 110kcal/468kJ; Protein 20g; Carbohydrate 2.8g, of which sugars 1.1g; Fat 2.3g, of which saturates 0.5g; Cholesterol 281mg; Calcium 43mg; Fibre 0.6g; Sodium 943mg.

# INDONESIAN DEEP-FRIED SPRING ROLLS

*MADE WITH A CRÊPE-STYLE BATTER USING RICE FLOUR, THESE INDONESIAN SPRING ROLLS ARE PACKED WITH VEGETABLES AND STRIPS OF CHICKEN AND THEN DIPPED IN KECAP MANIS, WHICH IS OFTEN SPIKED WITH CHILLIES. EXTRA CHILLIES, SEEDED AND THINLY SLICED, CAN ALSO BE SERVED ON THE SIDE.*

SERVES THREE TO FOUR

INGREDIENTS
  30ml/2 tbsp palm or corn oil
  2–3 garlic cloves, finely chopped
  225g/8oz chicken breast fillets,
    cut into fine strips
  225g/8oz fresh prawns
    (shrimp), shelled
  2 leeks, cut into matchsticks
  2 carrots, cut into matchsticks
  ½ green cabbage, finely shredded
  175g/6oz fresh beansprouts
  30ml/2 tbsp fish sauce
  30ml/2 tbsp kecap manis
    (Indonesian sweet soy sauce)
  1 egg, lightly beaten
  corn or vegetable oil, for deep-frying
  4 fresh red or green Thai chillies,
    or a mixture of both, seeded and
    finely sliced, to serve
For the spring roll wrappers
  115g/4oz/⅔ cup rice flour
  30ml/2 tbsp tapioca flour
    or cornflour (cornstarch)
  2 eggs, beaten
  15ml/1 tbsp palm or coconut oil
  about 400ml/14fl oz/1⅔ cups water
  salt
  corn or vegetable oil, for frying
For the dipping sauce
  about 200ml/7fl oz/¾ cup kecap
    manis (Indonesian sweet soy sauce)
  1 fresh red Thai chilli, seeded
    and chopped

**1** First make the spring roll wrappers. Sift the rice flour and tapioca flour into a bowl. Make a well in the centre, add the beaten eggs and oil into the well and gradually pour in the water, beating all the time until a smooth batter is formed. Season with salt and leave the batter to rest for 30 minutes.

**COOK'S TIP**

If you serve fresh chilli as a garnish or on the side, be aware that anyone eating with their fingers should be careful not to rub their eyes afterwards as the juice is an irritant.

**2** Heat a non-stick frying pan and wipe over a little oil. Using a small cup or ladle, add a little of the batter to the pan, tilting it to spread the batter evenly over the base. There should be enough batter to make 12 wrappers.

**3** Reduce the heat and cook gently on one side, until the batter is lightly browned and lifts at the edges. Lift the wrapper on to a plate and keep fresh under a clean, damp dish towel. Repeat with the remaining batter.

**4** To prepare the filling, heat 15ml/1 tbsp of the oil in a wok or large, heavy frying pan, stir in the garlic and fry gently until fragrant.

**5** Add the chicken and prawns and stir-fry for 2–3 minutes, until just cooked. Transfer to a plate and return the wok to the heat.

**6** Add the remaining oil to the wok, then add the leeks, carrots and cabbage and stir-fry for 2–3 minutes. Toss in the beansprouts and stir-fry for a further 1–2 minutes.

**7** Add the fish sauce and kecap manis and return the chicken and prawns to the pan, then toss until all the ingredients are thoroughly combined and coated in the sauce. Transfer the mixture to a plate and leave to cool.

**8** To fill the spring rolls, place a wrapper on a flat surface and drop a heaped spoonful of the filling on the side nearest to you. Spread the filling to form a log, then roll the edge nearest to you over the mixture, tuck in the sides and continue rolling the wrapper away from you. When you get to the far side, moisten it with a little of the beaten egg to seal the seam. Repeat to make 12 spring rolls.

**9** Before frying the spring rolls, quickly prepare the dipping sauce. Pour the kecap manis into a serving bowl, stir in the chopped chilli, and place the bowl next to the serving dish for the spring rolls.

**10** In a wok or heavy pan, heat enough oil for deep-frying. Carefully lower one or two spring rolls at a time into the pan and sizzle gently for 3–4 minutes, until golden brown and crisp. Using a slotted spoon, remove from the pan and drain on kitchen paper.

**11** Transfer the crisp rolls to the serving dish and serve immediately, with the dipping sauce and sliced chillies on the side for those who appreciate some extra heat.

**Per Portion** Energy 585kcal/2446kJ; Protein 35.4g; Carbohydrate 43.5g, of which sugars 7.2g; Fat 43.2g, of which saturates 4.5g; Cholesterol 292mg; Calcium 170mg; Fibre 5.1g; Sodium 744mg.

# MEATBALLS WITH TOASTED COCONUT

*A GREAT FAVOURITE AT INDONESIAN BUFFET SPREADS AND STREET STALLS, THESE MEATBALLS ARE VERSATILE AND TASTY. THE TASTY, BITESIZE BALLS CAN BE SERVED AS AN APPETIZER WITH A DRINK, AS A SNACK DIPPED IN KECAP MANIS, OR AS A MAIN DISH WITH RICE AND A TANGY SALAD.*

SERVES FOUR

INGREDIENTS
  5ml/1 tsp coriander seeds
  5ml/1 tsp cumin seeds
  175g/6oz freshly grated coconut
    or desiccated (dry unsweetened
    shredded) coconut
  15ml/1 tbsp coconut oil
  4 shallots, finely chopped
  2 garlic cloves, finely chopped
  1–2 fresh red chillies, seeded and
    finely chopped
  350g/12oz lean minced (ground) beef
  beaten egg (if necessary)
  rice flour, to coat
  corn oil, for shallow frying
  salt and ground black pepper
To serve
  1 lime, quartered
  kecap manis (Indonesian sweet
    soy sauce)

**1** In a small, heavy pan, dry-fry the coriander and cumin seeds until they give off a nutty aroma. Using a mortar and pestle or electric spice grinder, grind the roasted seeds to a powder.

**2** In the same pan, dry-fry the coconut until it begins to colour and give off a nutty aroma. Transfer the coconut to a plate and leave to cool.

**3** Heat the coconut oil in the same pan, stir in the shallots, garlic and chillies and fry until fragrant and beginning to colour. Transfer them to a plate to cool.

**4** Put the beef into a bowl and add the ground spices, all but 2–3 tbsp of the toasted coconut and the shallot mixture. Season the beef mixture with salt and pepper. Mix all the ingredients together, adding a little beaten egg, only if necessary, to bind the mixture together.

**5** Knead the mixture and mould it into little balls, not bigger than a fresh apricot. Roll the balls in rice flour to coat them.

**6** Heat a thin layer of corn oil in a large frying pan and fry the meatballs for about 5 minutes until they are golden brown all over. Drain on kitchen paper and arrange on a serving dish. Sprinkle the reserved coconut over them, and serve with the lime wedges for squeezing and kecap manis for drizzling over them.

**Per Portion** Energy 559kcal/2312kJ; Protein 20.2g; Carbohydrate 8g, of which sugars 3.7g; Fat 49.6g, of which saturates 30.4g; Cholesterol 53mg; Calcium 23mg; Fibre 6.3g; Sodium 83mg.

# RICE AND NOODLES

Rice and noodles in their many and varied guises form the
basis of meals throughout South-east Asia. The dishes in this
chapter include substantial meals as well as beautiful side
dishes to accompany curries or stir-fries. These form some of
the most popular dishes of Indonesia and no feast or family
meal would be complete without them.

# FESTIVE YELLOW RICE

*Vibrant yellow and rich in taste, this Indonesian rice dish is traditionally served during festive occasions, when it is often heaped up high on a platter to impress the waiting diners. Usually made with medium grain rice and coloured yellow with turmeric, this is a stunning rice dish that will complement any meal.*

SERVES FOUR

INGREDIENTS

450g/1lb/2¼ cups long grain rice
30ml/2 tbsp vegetable
  or sesame oil
2–3 shallots, finely chopped
2 garlic cloves, finely chopped
400ml/14fl oz/1⅔ cups coconut milk
450ml/¾ pint/scant 2 cups water
10ml/2 tsp ground turmeric
3–4 fresh curry leaves
salt and ground black pepper
2 fresh red chillies, seeded and
  finely sliced, to garnish

**1** Put the rice in a sieve (strainer), rinse under cold running water until the water runs clear, then drain. Heat the oil in a heavy pan, stir in the shallots and garlic and fry until just beginning to colour. Stir in the rice until coated in the oil.

**2** Add the coconut milk, water, turmeric, curry leaves, 2.5ml/½ tsp salt and pepper to the pan. Bring to the boil, then lower the heat, cover and simmer gently for 15–20 minutes, until all the liquid has been absorbed.

**3** Turn off the heat, cover the pan with a lid and leave the rice to steam for a further 10–15 minutes. Fluff up the rice with a fork and serve hot, garnished with red chillies.

**COOK'S TIP**
Allowing the rice to steam dry once all the liquid has been absorbed produces grains that are light and fluffy.

**Per Portion** Energy 487kcal/2035kJ; Protein 9.1g; Carbohydrate 96.5g, of which sugars 5.8g; Fat 6.7g, of which saturates 0.9g; Cholesterol 0mg; Calcium 70mg; Fibre 0.8g; Sodium 122mg.

# INDONESIAN FRIED RICE

*DESPITE ITS DUTCH ORIGINS, THIS DISH OF FRIED RICE (NASI GORENG) IS ONE OF INDONESIA'S NATIONAL FAVOURITES. GENERALLY MADE WITH LEFTOVER COOKED GRAINS, THE FRIED RICE IS SERVED WITH CRISPY SHALLOTS AND CHILLIES, OR ELSE TOSSED WITH PRAWNS (SHRIMP) OR CRAB MEAT AND CHOPPED VEGETABLES. A FRIED EGG ON TOP OF THE DOMED RICE COMPLETES THE DISH.*

### SERVES FOUR

INGREDIENTS
  ½ cucumber
  45ml/3 tbsp vegetable or groundnut
    (peanut) oil
  4 shallots, finely chopped
  4 garlic cloves, finely chopped
  3–4 fresh red chillies, seeded
    and chopped
  45ml/3 tbsp kecap manis
    (Indonesian sweet soy sauce)
  15ml/1 tbsp tomato purée (paste)
  350g/12oz/1¾ cups cooked
    long grain rice
  4 eggs

**1** Cut the cucumber in half lengthways and scoop out the seeds. Cut the flesh into thin sticks. Put aside.

**2** In a wok, heat 30ml/2 tbsp of the oil, stir in the shallots, garlic and chillies and fry until they begin to colour. Add the kecap manis and tomato purée and stir for 2 minutes until thick, to form a sauce. Toss in the rice and heat for 5 minutes until well flavoured and hot.

**3** Meanwhile, in a large frying pan, heat the remaining oil over a medium heat and crack the eggs into it. Fry for 1–2 minutes until the whites are cooked but the yolks remain runny. Reduce the heat to a minimum while you quickly prepare the servings of rice.

**4** Spoon the rice into four deep bowls. Alternatively, use one bowl as a mould to invert each portion of rice on to individual plates, then lift off the bowl to reveal the mound of rice beneath. Place a fried egg on top of each and garnish with the cucumber sticks.

**Per Portion** Energy 273kcal/1146kJ; Protein 9.9g; Carbohydrate 33g, of which sugars 4.7g; Fat 12.3g, of which saturates 2.5g; Cholesterol 190mg; Calcium 67mg; Fibre 1.1g; Sodium 884mg.

# MIXED VEGETABLE RICE

*This is a dish that crosses many borders that features throughout Indonesia as well as in Malaysia and Singapore. Campur (pronounced 'cham-poor') simply means 'mixed', and the dish can be adapted to include all kinds of savoury ingredients with the hot rice. It is particularly good if served with a spicy relish or sambal.*

**2** Blanch the beans in boiling water for 2 minutes. Drain, cool and dice finely.

**3** Peel the cucumber and remove the seeds. Cut into fine dice.

**4** Chop the hard-boiled eggs.

**5** Just before serving, toss all the ingredients together and adjust the seasoning. Serve with Cucumber and Pineapple Relish on the side.

**COOK'S TIP**
When you cook the rice, crumble in a vegetarian stock cube. This will give the finished dish a well-rounded flavour.

SERVES FOUR

INGREDIENTS
   200g/7oz/1 cup jasmine rice
   2 yard-long beans or 5 green beans
   ¼ cucumber
   2 hard-boiled eggs
   3 fresh red chillies, seeded
    and chopped
   4 lime leaves, finely shredded
   5ml/1 tsp salt
   1.5ml/¼ tsp ground black pepper
   30ml/2 tbsp fresh lime juice
   2 tomatoes, chopped
   45ml/3 tbsp Cucumber and Pineapple
    Relish (see page 21)

**1** Put the rice in a sieve (strainer), rinse under cold running water until the water runs clear, then put it in a pan and cover with water up to 4cm/1½in above the rice. Cook for 12–15 minutes until tender.

**Per Portion** Energy 199kcal/834kJ; Protein 4.6g; Carbohydrate 43.4g, of which sugars 6.6g; Fat 0.7g, of which saturates 0.1g; Cholesterol 105mg; Calcium 23mg; Fibre 1.6g; Sodium 232mg.

# JUNGLE RICE

*THE NAME OF THIS DISH ALLUDES NOT SO MUCH TO TRIBAL COOKING AS TO THE WILD GREENS AND HERBS FOUND IN TROPICAL FORESTED AREAS. ORIGINALLY, THIS DISH OF INDIGENOUS EDIBLE PLANTS WAS COOKED BY PEOPLE LIVING ON THE FRINGES OF INDONESIAN JUNGLES. TODAY, IT IS LIKELY TO BE PREPARED WITH GARDEN VEGETABLES. THE MAIN FLAVOUR COMES FROM THE SHRIMP PASTE AND CHILLIES.*

### SERVES FOUR

INGREDIENTS
  350g/12oz/1¾ cups jasmine rice
  1 whole mackerel or snapper
  30ml/2 tbsp vegetable oil
  2 eggs
  4 shallots, sliced
  4 garlic cloves, sliced
  2 fresh green chillies, sliced
  2 yard-long or 5 green beans, finely
    diced
  2 lime leaves, finely shredded
  small sprig fresh sweet basil, chopped
  6 fresh mint leaves, shredded
  5ml/1 tsp salt

For the sambal
  50g/2oz terasi (Indonesian shrimp
    paste), toasted
  5 fresh red chillies, finely chopped
  juice of 2 limes

**1** Grind all the sambal ingredients with a mortar and pestle until smooth, and set aside.

**2** Put the jasmine rice in a sieve (strainer), rinse under cold water until the water runs clear, then put it in a pan and cover with water up to 4cm/1½in above the rice. Bring to the boil and cook for 12–15 minutes until tender.

**VARIATION**
You can use the equivalent amount of Shallot and Lemon Grass Sambal (see page 18) in place of this sambal for an even more tangy dish.

**3** Clean the mackerel or snapper, pat dry with kitchen paper, then grill (broil) for about 7 minutes on each side until cooked through.

**4** Carefully debone the fish and flake the flesh into a bowl. Discard the skin and bones.

**5** Heat the oil and fry the eggs, then remove to a plate.

**6** While the rice is still warm, mix in the prepared vegetables, fish, lime leaves and herbs, and mix in the shrimp paste sambal to taste. Place in a large serving bowl, topped with the eggs.

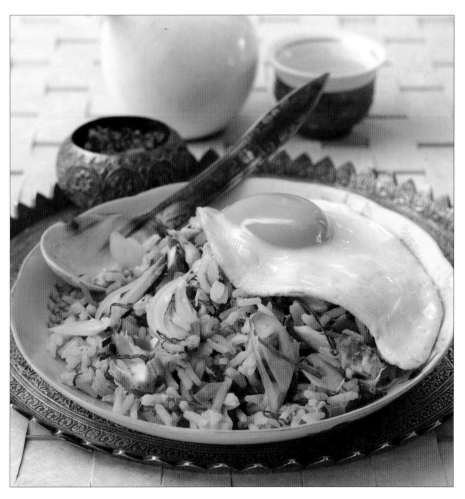

**Per Portion** Energy 487kcal/2032kJ; Protein 16.9g; Carbohydrate 72.7g, of which sugars 0.8g; Fat 14g, of which saturates 2.5g; Cholesterol 112mg; Calcium 46mg; Fibre 1.1g; Sodium 547mg.

# PADANG CHICKEN RICE WITH LEMON GRASS

*THIS DISH IS BELIEVED TO HAIL FROM THE PADANG REGION OF INDONESIA AND IS USUALLY COOKED FOR FESTIVE OCCASIONS. TRADITIONALLY, A WHOLE CHICKEN IS USED, BUT THIS RECIPE USES JUST CHICKEN FILLETS FOR CONVENIENCE. IT IS A MOST APPETIZING ONE-POT MEAL, AROMATIC WITH LEMON GRASS, NUTMEG, MACE AND GALANGAL.*

**2** Cook the rice according to the packet instructions but with the nutmeg, pepper and mace. When cooked, remove the mace and keep the rice warm.

**3** Place the chicken in small pot with the water, lemon grass, galangal, lime leaves, garlic and salt. Cook for 10 minutes until the liquid has almost entirely been absorbed or has evaporated.

**4** Remove the lemon grass and lime leaves (or leave for a rustic presentation).

## SERVES FOUR

### INGREDIENTS
    60ml/4 tbsp vegetable oil
    8 shallots, peeled and sliced
    400g/14oz/2 cups long grain
      or basmati rice
    pinch of grated nutmeg
    2.5ml/½ tsp ground black pepper
    2 small pieces of mace
    2 chicken breast fillets, thinly sliced
    300ml/½ pint/1¼ cups water
    2 lemon grass stalks, 5cm/2in
      of root end bruised
    5ml/1 tsp ground galangal
    3 lime leaves
    2 garlic cloves
    5ml/1 tsp salt

**1** Heat the oil and fry the shallots until crisp and golden brown. Remove and set aside on crumpled kitchen paper.

**COOK'S TIP**
Fried shallots are required for many Indonesian dishes, so cook a large batch, drain, then store in an airtight container.

**5** Mix the chicken with the cooked rice and stir well to incorporate the flavours. Serve garnished with the fried shallots.

**Per Portion** Energy 557kcal/2328kJ; Protein 26.3g; Carbohydrate 83.1g, of which sugars 1.4g; Fat 12.9g, of which saturates 1.6g; Cholesterol 53mg; Calcium 36mg; Fibre 0.4g; Sodium 538mg.

# OIL RICE <u>WITH</u> CHICKEN

*THIS IS A FESTIVE TAKE ON THE COCONUT RICE USUALLY EATEN IN INDONESIA AND IS FRAGRANT WITH THE SCENT OF COCONUT OIL. SOME VERSIONS USE GHEE OR CLARIFIED BUTTER, BUT THIS INTENSELY FLAVOURED FAT CAN DISTRACT FROM THE AROMA OF RICE AND CHICKEN, ENDING UP ALMOST LIKE AN INDIAN PILAU RICE. COCONUT OIL IS A SOLID FAT THAT LOOKS LIKE LARD.*

SERVES FOUR

INGREDIENTS
   350g/12oz glutinous rice
   45ml/3 tbsp coconut oil
   5ml/1 tsp salt
   1 large banana leaf, about
      30cm/12in square
   2 chicken breasts, cut into
      bitesize pieces
   2 salam leaves (Indonesian bay leaves)
   105ml/7 tbsp coconut milk
   pinch of cinnamon powder
   2.5ml/½ tsp salt
   2 fresh green chillies

**4** Blanch the banana leaf in boiling water, then cut it and line the basket. Add the rice and top with more bamboo leaf 'lid' before closing the steamer lid.

**5** Steam for 20 minutes, then taste a few grains. If there is no hard edge, the rice is done. If there still is a hard edge, steam for a little longer.

**6** While the rice is steaming, combine the chicken with the salam leaves, coconut milk, cinnamon, salt and whole chillies, and simmer in a pan or wok for 10 minutes. During the last 5 minutes of the rice being cooked, remove the bamboo lid and pile the chicken on top. Finish cooking both together, to let the juices mingle. Serve in warmed bowls.

**1** Soak the glutinous rice for at least 2 hours or overnight in water for a softer consistency, as this is a dense grain.

**2** On the day of preparation, drain the rice until it is just moist. Most of the water will have been absorbed.

**3** Melt the coconut oil in a small pan, add the salt and and stir to blend well. Pour over the rice and transfer to a bamboo steamer.

**Per Portion** Energy 474kcal/1984kJ; Protein 24.7g; Carbohydrate 71.2g, of which sugars 1.3g; Fat 9.6g, of which saturates 7.4g; Cholesterol 53mg; Calcium 29mg; Fibre 0g; Sodium 811mg.

# INDONESIAN STIR-FRIED NOODLES

*ORIGINALLY FROM CHINA, STIR-FRIED NOODLES HAVE BECOME AS POPULAR AS STIR-FRIED RICE AT STREET STALLS THROUGHOUT INDONESIA. THIS DISH IS EASY TO PREPARE IN ADVANCE – THE PAR-BOILED NOODLES WILL KEEP FOR HOURS BEFORE THE FINAL PAN-COOKING STAGE. AS IN MANY INDONESIAN RECIPES, THE GARNISH IS ESSENTIAL FOR ADDING FLAVOUR.*

### SERVES FOUR

INGREDIENTS

450g/1lb fresh egg noodles
60ml/4 tbsp palm, groundnut
  (peanut) or corn oil, plus extra
  for frying
2 shallots, finely chopped
2–3 spring onions (scallions),
  finely chopped
2–3 garlic cloves, crushed
3–4 fresh Thai chillies, seeded and
  finely chopped
15ml/1 tbsp terasi
  (Indonesian shrimp paste)
15ml/1 tbsp tomato purée (paste)
15–30ml/1–2 tbsp kecap manis
  (Indonesian sweet soy sauce)
4 eggs
salt
To garnish
15ml/1 tbsp palm or corn oil
3–4 shallots, thinly sliced

**1** First prepare the garnish. Heat the oil in a heavy pan, stir in the shallots and fry until deep golden brown. Drain on kitchen paper and put aside.

**2** Fill a deep pan with water and bring it to the boil. Drop in the egg noodles, untangling them with chopsticks, and cook for about 3 minutes until tender but still firm to the bite. Drain and refresh under cold running water.

**3** Heat 30ml/2 tbsp of the oil in a wok or large, heavy frying pan and fry the chopped shallots, spring onions, garlic and chillies until fragrant. Add the terasi and continue to cook until the mixture darkens.

**4** Toss the noodles into the pan, making sure that they are thoroughly coated in the mixture.

**5** Add the tomato purée and kecap manis, toss thoroughly, and cook for 2–3 minutes.

**6** Season the noodles with salt to taste. Divide the noodles between four warmed dishes and keep warm.

**7** Heat the remaining oil in a large frying pan and crack the eggs into it. Fry for 1–2 minutes until the whites are cooked but the yolks remain runny.

**8** Place one fried egg on top of each noodle serving and sprinkle the fried shallots over the top. Serve immediately while hot.

**Per Portion** Energy 549kcal/2317kJ; Protein 20.5g; Carbohydrate 82.9g, of which sugars 3.9g; Fat 17.6g, of which saturates 4.5g; Cholesterol 224mg; Calcium 68mg; Fibre 3.7g; Sodium 549mg.

# RICE WITH MEAT AND PLANTAINS

*THERE IS MORE THAN A LITTLE CREOLE-CARIBBEAN INFLUENCE IN THIS INDONESIA DISH, PLANTAINS BEING A HALLMARK OF THAT CUISINE. THEY MAY LOOK LIKE LARGE BANANAS BUT ARE REGARDED AS A SWEET VEGETABLE RATHER THAN A DESSERT FRUIT. VERY FIRM IN TEXTURE, PLANTAINS RARELY RIPEN TO SOFTNESS AND HAVE TO BE COOKED TO BE REALLY EDIBLE.*

SERVES FOUR

INGREDIENTS
    45ml/3 tbsp olive oil
    5 shallots, sliced
    3 garlic cloves, crushed
    2 tomatoes, quartered
    200g/7oz minced (ground) beef
    200g/7oz minced (ground) pork
    30ml/2 tbsp soy sauce
    15ml/1 tbsp vinegar
    50g/2oz/⅓ cup sultanas
      (golden raisins)
    2.5ml/½ tsp salt
    2.5ml/½ tsp ground black pepper
    50g/2oz/⅓ cup corn kernels
    400g/14oz/2 cups long grain rice
    60ml/4 tbsp vegetable oil
    200g/7oz plantains, sliced diagonally
      into 2cm/¾in slices
    4 eggs
    fresh mint or coriander (cilantro)
      leaves, to garnish

**1** Heat the olive oil in a large wok and fry the shallots until light brown. Add the garlic and fry for 1 minute, then add the tomatoes, beef, pork, soy sauce and vinegar and stir over a medium heat for about 8 minutes, until the meats are cooked through.

**2** Add the sultanas, salt, pepper and corn and stir-fry for 1 minute. Remove the wok from the heat and set aside.

**3** Meanwhile, boil or steam the rice according to the packet instructions. When it is ready, keep it warm.

**4** Heat the vegetable oil in a frying pan and fry the plantain slices until they are slightly caramelized. Remove with a slotted spoon and drain any excess oil on crumpled kitchen paper.

**5** Fry the eggs 'sunny side up' in the same oil, then set aside. The yolks should still be runny, and the whites completely set.

**6** Press the rice into a small dessert or cereal bowl for each person, then unmould it on to a warmed plate. Top it with a fried egg and serve the cooked meat mixture and the plantains on the side. Garnish with the fresh herbs.

**VARIATION**
If you are unable to get plantains you could use sweet potato for a colourful and flavoursome alternative. Par-boil slices of sweet potato for 3 minutes, then cook them in the same way as you would the plantains.

**Per Portion** Energy 929kcal/3878kJ; Protein 35.2g; Carbohydrate 110.7g, of which sugars 16.2g; Fat 38.8g, of which saturates 9.2g; Cholesterol 253mg; Calcium 80mg; Fibre 1.9g; Sodium 721mg.

# NOODLES AND RICE WITH TOFU AND BEANSPROUT BROTH

*THIS DISH IS KNOWN IN INDONESIA AS NASI MI. THE CUSTOM IS TO SERVE THE NOODLES, RICE, TOFU, BROTH AND SAMBAL INDIVIDUALLY. EACH PERSON THEN SPOONS RICE INTO A BOWL, FOLLOWED BY THE TOFU AND SAMBAL, THEN A LADLEFUL OF BROTH, WITH THE NOODLES EATEN SEPARATELY.*

### SERVES FOUR TO SIX

INGREDIENTS
    corn or vegetable oil, for deep-frying
    250g/9oz tofu block
    225g/8oz/1⅛ cup jasmine rice
For the broth
    15ml/1 tbsp palm or corn oil
    2 garlic cloves, finely chopped
    1–2 fresh red or green chillies,
       seeded and finely chopped
    1 lemon grass stalk, finely chopped
    45ml/3 tbsp soy sauce
    2 litres/3½ pints/8 cups
       chicken stock
    450g/1lb fresh mung beansprouts
    ground black pepper
For the noodles
    30ml/2 tbsp palm or corn oil
    4 shallots, finely sliced
    2 garlic cloves, finely chopped
    450g/1lb shelled prawns (shrimp)
    30ml/2 tbsp kecap manis
       (Indonesian sweet soy sauce)
    500g/1¼lb fresh egg noodles or
       225g/8oz dried egg noodles,
       soaked in warm water for 5 minutes
       until softened
To serve
    4–6 spring onions (scallions),
       finely sliced
    chilli sambal

**1** Cut the tofu into 4 rectangular pieces.

**2** Heat enough oil in a wok or heavy pan for deep-frying. Add the tofu pieces and fry for 2–3 minutes, until golden brown on both sides, then drain on kitchen paper. Cut into thin slices, and place on a plate. Set aside.

**3** Put the rice in a sieve (strainer), rinse under cold running water until the water runs clear, then drain. Transfer the rice to a pan and add about 600ml/1 pint/2½ cups water to cover the rice.

**4** Bring the rice to the boil, then reduce the heat and simmer gently for about 15 minutes, until all the water has been absorbed. Turn off the heat, cover the pan and leave to steam for 10–15 minutes.

**COOK'S TIP**
Although the tradition is to serve each ingredient in separate bowls, nasi mi is often served as a self-contained meal in a single dish at many street stalls.

**5** Meanwhile, make the broth. Heat the palm or corn oil in a wok or heavy pan, stir in the chopped garlic, chillies and lemon grass and stir-fry until fragrant and softened.

**6** Add 15ml/1 tbsp of the soy sauce to the mixture in the pan and pour in the chicken stock. Bring to the boil, then reduce the heat and simmer for 10–15 minutes.

**7** Season the broth with the remaining soy sauce and pepper and stir in the beansprouts. Turn off the heat and keep warm in a covered pan over a very low heat or in a casserole in the oven.

**8** Finally, prepare the noodles. Heat the oil in a wok, stir in the shallots and garlic and fry until they begin to colour. Toss in the prawns and cook for 2 minutes, then stir in the kecap manis with 15–30ml/1–2 tbsp water. Add the noodles, season and toss well.

**9** Divide the rice and noodles into individual warmed dishes and serve with the tofu, a bowl of spring onions, chilli sambal and a bowl of the steaming hot broth, so that everyone can help themselves.

**VARIATION**
If you don't have or can't find any kecap manis, you can substitute the same quantity of dark soy sauce mixed with a little sugar.

**Per Portion** Energy 690kcal/2900kJ; Protein 32.6g; Carbohydrate 97g, of which sugars 5.9g; Fat 20.7g, of which saturates 3.6g; Cholesterol 171mg; Calcium 328mg; Fibre 4.2g; Sodium 833mg.

# FISH AND SHELLFISH

*With the islands' endless miles of idyllic coastline, it is no surprise that fish and shellfish form an important part of the Indonesian diet. In this chapter you will encounter special dishes that make the best of the local fishermen's catch. Don't miss out on the fiery Sumatran favourite, Sardines in Spicy Coconut Milk, for an authentic taste of the region.*

# FISH CROQUETTES

*THIS DISH IS KNOWN IN INDONESIA AS BEGEDEL IKAN. THE WORD BEGEDEL IS OF DUTCH HERITAGE, BUT THE FRENCH WORD 'CROQUETTE' IS A MORE FAMILIAR TERM TO MOST WESTERNERS. POTATOES ARE USUALLY INVOLVED, ALTHOUGH IN SOME REGIONS ONLY FRESH BREADCRUMBS ARE USED. VERSIONS THAT USE SEAFOOD, BEEF OR PORK EXIST, AND EVEN CANNED FISH CAN BE USED.*

**3** Lightly beat the eggs and mix with the milk. Add the potatoes and fish and mix well. Stir in the flour to make a thick mixture. Add the salt, ground cloves, black pepper and spring onion.

**4** Shape the mixture into balls, each the size of a plum, and flatten a little. Dust with flour.

**5** Heat enough oil for deep-frying and fry the croquettes in batches until golden brown. Drain on crumpled kitchen paper.

**6** Serve with a bowl of your favourite chilli sauce, for dipping.

SERVES FOUR

INGREDIENTS
    600g/1lb 6oz potatoes
    450g/1lb cod or halibut
    2 eggs
    105ml/7 tbsp milk
    40g/1½oz plain (all-purpose) flour,
        plus extra for dusting
    5ml/1 tsp salt
    pinch of ground cloves
    2.5ml/½ tsp ground black pepper
    1 spring onion (scallion), white part
        only, finely chopped
    vegetable oil for deep-frying
    chilli sauce, to serve

**1** Boil the potatoes until well done, then drain, peel (when cool enough to handle) and mash.

**2** Poach the fish in 400ml/14fl oz/ 1⅔ cups water for 10 minutes. Remove the fish using a slotted spoon and place on a plate. Flake or mash the flesh, removing any bones as you go, then discard the poaching water.

**VARIATION**
Other types of white fish can be used. Canned tuna also works well, and saves cooking time.

**Per Portion** Energy 402kcal/1684kJ; Protein 28.1g; Carbohydrate 33.2g, of which sugars 3.3g; Fat 18.3g, of which saturates 3g; Cholesterol 148mg; Calcium 79mg; Fibre 1.8g; Sodium 622mg.

# FRIED ANCHOVIES AND PEANUTS

*IN THE REGION OF PADANG, MEALS ARE THOUGHT INCOMPLETE WITHOUT FRIED ANCHOVIES, WHICH ARE OFTEN COMBINED WITH PEANUTS FOR A CRUNCHY KICK. THE PEANUTS USED ARE A SMALL, RED-SKINNED VARIETY AND ARE TRADITIONALLY COOKED WITH THEIR SKINS ON. DRIED ANCHOVIES USUALLY HAVE A FINE COATING OF FLOURY DUST ON THEM. SHAKE THIS OFF BEFORE FRYING.*

SERVES FOUR

INGREDIENTS

150g/5oz red-skinned, raw peanuts
75ml/5 tbsp vegetable oil
150g/5oz dried anchovies
100ml/3½fl oz/⅓ cup coconut milk
30g/2 tbsp Shallot and Lemon Grass
   Sambal (see page 18)
15ml/1 tbsp lime juice
5ml/1 tsp sugar

**4** Fry for 1 minute, then add the coconut milk, sambal, lime juice and sugar. There is no need to add any salt as the sambal is already seasoned.

**5** Stir to mix, then serve warm or cold.

**1** Dry-fry the peanuts in a warm wok for 10–15 minutes, until the skins begin to blister. Remove the peanuts from the wok and set aside.

**2** Heat the oil in the wok and fry the dried anchovies until crisp and brown. Drain on kitchen paper.

**3** Pour off all but 2 tbsp of the oil and return the nuts and anchovies to the wok.

**COOK'S TIP**
Small dried anchovies are ideal for this recipe. Larger ones should be used for stock and stews rather than snacking.

**Per Portion** Energy 419kcal/1738kJ; Protein 19.3g; Carbohydrate 6.4g, of which sugars 3.9g; Fat 35.4g, of which saturates 5.6g; Cholesterol 24mg; Calcium 145mg; Fibre 2.4g; Sodium 1526mg.

# SARDINES COOKED IN SPICY COCONUT MILK WITH HERBS

*A FISH DISH BASED ON COCONUT MILK, REMPAH~REMPAH VARIES FROM REGION TO REGION. IN NORTHERN SUMATRA, WHERE THE TOLERANCE FOR CHILLIES AND SPICE IS HIGH, THIS DISH IS PARTICULARLY FIERY BUT IS TEMPERED BY THE INCLUSION OF LOCALLY GROWN HERBS. AS A SUBSTITUTE FOR THE LOCAL HERBS, WHICH ARE NOT AVAILABLE IN THE WEST, THIS RECIPE USES FRESH MINT, BASIL AND FLAT LEAF PARSLEY INSTEAD.*

## SERVES FOUR

### INGREDIENTS

- 6–8 fresh red chillies, according to taste, seeded and chopped
- 4 shallots, chopped
- 4 garlic cloves, chopped
- 1 lemon grass stalk, chopped
- 25g/1oz fresh galangal, chopped
- 30ml/2 tbsp coconut or palm oil
- 10ml/2 tsp coriander seeds
- 5ml/1 tsp cumin seeds
- 5ml/1 tsp fennel seeds
- 1 small bunch fresh mint leaves, finely chopped
- 1 small bunch fresh flat leaf parsley, finely chopped
- 15ml/1 tbsp palm sugar (jaggery)
- 15ml/1 tbsp tamarind paste
- 4 sardines or small mackerel, gutted, kept whole
- 300ml/½ pint/1¼ cups coconut milk
- salt and ground black pepper

To serve
- steamed rice or sago
- 1 large bunch fresh flat leaf parsley
- fresh basil leaves

**1** Using a mortar and pestle, pound the chillies, shallots, garlic, lemon grass and galangal to a paste.

**2** Heat the oil in a wok or wide, heavy pan, stir in the coriander, cumin and fennel seeds and fry until they give off a nutty aroma. Add the paste and stir until it becomes fragrant and golden in colour. Add the chopped mint and parsley and stir for 1 minute, then add the sugar and tamarind paste.

**3** Carefully place the fish in the pan, coating them in the paste, and pour in the coconut milk. Bring to the boil, then reduce the heat and cook gently for 10–15 minutes, until the fish is tender. Season the sauce with salt and pepper to taste.

**4** Cover the bottom of a warmed serving dish with parsley and place the fish on top, then spoon the sauce over the top. Serve with a bowl of steamed rice or sago and stalks of fresh parsley and basil leaves.

**Per Portion** Energy 287kcal/1199kJ; Protein 22.8g; Carbohydrate 11g, of which sugars 10.2g; Fat 17.2g, of which saturates 3.7g; Cholesterol 0mg; Calcium 167mg; Fibre 2.1g; Sodium 213mg.

# ·FISH COOKED IN BANANA LEAVES

*COOKING FISH IN BANANA LEAVES IS A DELIGHTFUL METHOD THAT CAN BE FOUND THROUGHOUT SOUTH-EAST ASIA. THE BANANA LEAVES IMPART THEIR OWN FLAVOUR TO THE FISH, WHICH REMAINS BEAUTIFULLY SUCCULENT AND FRAGRANT WITHIN ITS NATURAL WRAPPING.*

SERVES FOUR

INGREDIENTS
    500g/1¼lb fresh fish fillets,
      cut into chunks
    juice of 2 limes
    4–6 shallots, chopped
    2 fresh red chillies, seeded
      and chopped
    25g/1oz fresh root ginger,
      finey chopped
    15g/½oz fresh turmeric,
      finely chopped
    2 lemon grass stalks, chopped
    3–4 candlenuts, crushed
    10ml/2 tsp palm sugar (jaggery)
    salt
    1–2 banana leaves, cut into
      4 big squares
To serve
    cooked rice
    chilli sambal

**1** In a large bowl, toss the fish fillets in the lime juice then leave to marinate at room temperature for 10–15 minutes.

**2** Meanwhile, using a mortar and pestle, pound the shallots, chillies, ginger, turmeric and lemon grass to a coarse paste. Add the candlenuts and sugar and season with salt. Transfer the paste to the bowl with the fish and toss to coat the fish in it.

**3** Place the banana leaves on a flat surface and divide the fish mixture equally among them.

**4** Tuck in the sides and fold over the ends to form neat parcels and secure with string.

**5** Place the banana leaf parcels in a steamer and cook for 25–30 minutes until tender.

**6** Serve the fish parcels hot with rice and a chilli sambal.

**COOK'S TIP**
Banana leaves are available in South-east Asian, Chinese and African food shops, but if you cannot find banana leaves, use aluminium foil instead, and bake the fish parcels in the oven at 180°C/350°F/ Gas 4 instead of steaming them.

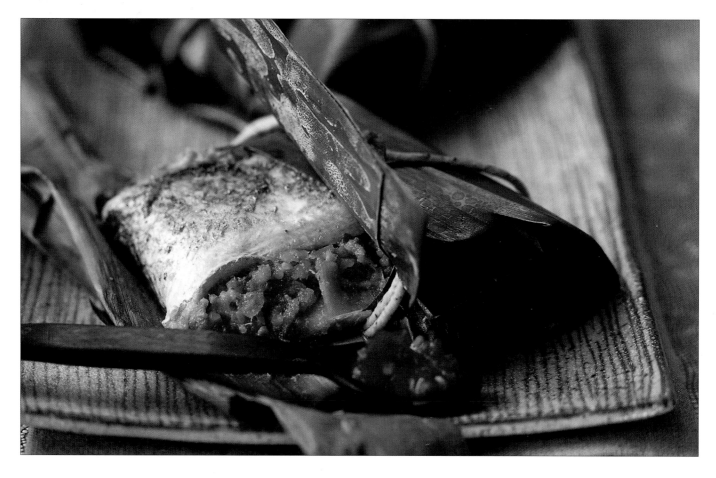

**Per Portion** Energy 225kcal/943kJ; Protein 27.6g; Carbohydrate 14.1g, of which sugars 10.4g; Fat 6.9g, of which saturates 1.2g; Cholesterol 58mg; Calcium 51mg; Fibre 2.5g; Sodium 79mg.

# CHARGRILLED FISH <sup>WITH</sup> SAMBAL BADJAK

*IN THE COASTAL REGIONS OF INDONESIA, GRILLING FISH OVER CHARCOAL IS A COMMON SIGHT IN THE TOURIST RESORTS, IN THE VILLAGES, ON THE BEACH AND BY THE ROADSIDE. THIS RECIPE IS VERSATILE ENOUGH TO USE WITH MOST FISH, SO JUST CHOOSE WHAT LOOKS BEST AT THE FISHMONGER.*

## SERVES FOUR

### INGREDIENTS

1 whole large sea fish, such as
    grouper, red snapper, sea bass,
    1 large piece of swordfish,
    or 4 whole smaller fish, such as
    sardines, gutted and cleaned
30ml/2 tbsp coconut oil
60ml/4 tbsp dark soy sauce
2 garlic cloves, crushed
juice of 1 lime
cooked rice and fresh coriander
    (cilantro) sprigs, to serve
For the sambal
    50g/2oz tamarind paste
    150ml/¼ pint/⅔ cup boiling water
    4 shallots, chopped
    4 garlic cloves, chopped
    4–6 fresh red chillies, seeded
        and chopped
    25g/1oz fresh galangal, chopped
    2 kaffir lime leaves, crumbled
    10ml/2 tsp terasi (Indonesian
        shrimp paste)
    10ml/2 tsp palm sugar (jaggery)
    30ml/2 tbsp coconut or palm oil

**1** Slash the fish at about 2.5cm/1in intervals with a sharp knife. Place in a shallow dish.

**2** In a small bowl, mix the coconut oil, soy sauce, garlic and lime juice together. Spoon the marinade over the fish and rub it into the skin and slashes. Leave for about 1 hour.

**3** Meanwhile, prepare the sambal. Put the tamarind paste in a bowl, pour over the boiling water and leave to soak for 30 minutes. Strain into a separate bowl, pressing the paste through a sieve (strainer). Discard the solids and put the tamarind juice aside.

**4** Using a mortar and pestle, pound the shallots, garlic, chillies, galangal and lime leaves to a coarse paste. Add the terasi and sugar and beat to combine.

**5** Heat the oil in a small wok, stir in the paste and fry for 2–3 minutes. Stir in the tamarind juice and boil until it reduces to a thick paste. Turn into a serving bowl.

**6** Prepare the barbecue. Place the fish on the rack and cook for 5 minutes on each side, depending on the size of fish, basting it with any leftover marinade. Transfer the fish to a serving plate, garnished with coriander, and serve with the sambal and cooked rice.

**Per Portion** Energy 359kcal/1507kJ; Protein 42.3g; Carbohydrate 11.8g, of which sugars 9.3g; Fat 16.4g, of which saturates 2.3g; Cholesterol 75mg; Calcium 117mg; Fibre 1.4g; Sodium 1263mg.

# CATFISH WITH A SPICY COCONUT SAUCE

*IN THIS POPULAR INDONESIAN DISH, CATFISH IS SIMPLY FRIED AND SERVED WITH A FRAGRANT AND SPICY SAUCE. MANY INDONESIAN COOKS MAKE UP JARS OF THE SPICE PASTE BASE GEDE, WHICH THEY KEEP FOR FLAVOURING MEAT, POULTRY AND FISH DISHES.*

### SERVES FOUR

INGREDIENTS
    200ml/7fl oz/¾ cup coconut milk
    30ml/2 tbsp coconut cream
    30ml/2 tbsp rice flour, tapioca flour
        or cornflour (cornstarch)
    5ml/1 tsp ground coriander
    8 fresh catfish fillets
    30ml/2 tbsp coconut, palm,
        groundnut (peanut) or corn oil
    salt and ground black pepper
    fresh coriander (cilantro) leaves,
        to garnish
To serve
    boiled rice
    1 lime, quartered
For the spice paste
    2 shallots, chopped
    2 garlic cloves, chopped
    2 fresh red chillies, seeded
        and chopped
    25g/1oz fresh galangal, chopped
    15g/½ oz fresh turmeric, chopped,
        or 2.5ml/½ tsp ground turmeric
    2–3 lemon grass stalks, chopped
    15ml/1 tbsp palm or groundnut
        (peanut) oil
    5ml/1 tsp terasi (Indonesian
        shrimp paste)
    15ml/1 tbsp tamarind paste
    5ml/1 tsp palm sugar (jaggery)

**1** Using a mortar and pestle or food processor, pound the shallots, garlic, chillies, galangal, turmeric and lemon grass to a paste.

**2** Heat the oil in a wok or heavy pan, stir in the paste and fry until it becomes fragrant and begins to colour. Add the terasi, tamarind paste and sugar and continue to stir until the paste darkens.

**3** Stir the coconut milk and cream into the spice paste and boil for about 10 minutes, until the milk and cream separate, leaving behind an oily paste. Season with salt and pepper to taste.

**4** Meanwhile, on a large plate, mix the flour with the coriander and season with salt and pepper. Toss the catfish fillets in the flour so that they are lightly coated all over.

**5** Heat the oil in a heavy frying pan and quickly fry the fillets for about 2 minutes on each side, until golden.

**6** Using a fish slice, transfer the catfish fillets to warmed dishes with helpings of rice in them. Spoon the coconut sauce over the fish and provide lime wedges for squeezing.

**COOK'S TIP**
Catfish is hugely popular in some areas of the world, but not readily found in many European stores and markets. If you cannot find it, or do not like catfish, use firm, plump fillets of sole or halibut instead.

**Per Portion** Energy 338kcal/1412kJ; Protein 38.1g; Carbohydrate 11.9g, of which sugars 4.9g; Fat 15.3g, of which saturates 5.7g; Cholesterol 92mg; Calcium 56mg; Fibre 0.9g; Sodium 190mg.

# SUMATRAN SOUR FISH AND STAR FRUIT STEW

*SOMEWHERE BETWEEN A STEW AND A SOUP, THIS REFRESHING DISH IS JUST ONE OF MANY VARIATIONS ON THE THEME OF SOUR FISH STEW FOUND THROUGHOUT SOUTH-EAST ASIA. THE STAR FRUIT ARE ADDED TOWARDS THE END OF COOKING SO THAT THE FRUIT RETAINS SOME BITE.*

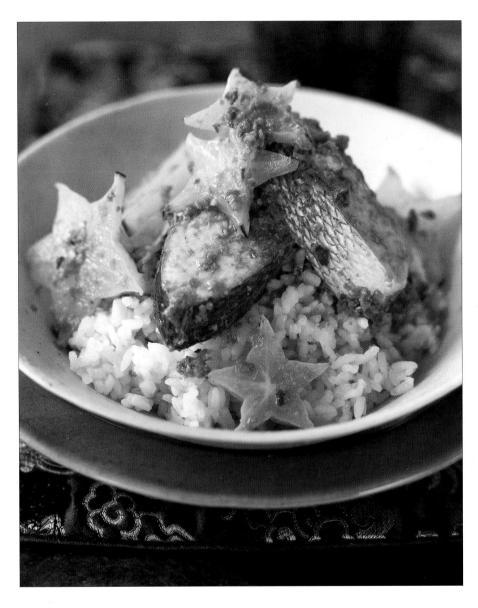

**1** Grind the spice paste ingredients to a coarse paste using a pestle and mortar or an electric food processor or blender. Heat the oil in a wok or wide, heavy pan, stir in the spice paste and fry until fragrant. Pour in the water and add the lemon grass and ginger. Bring to the boil, stirring all the time, then reduce the heat and simmer for 10 minutes.

**2** Slip the fish into the pan, making sure there is enough liquid to cover the fish and adding more water if necessary, then simmer gently for 3–4 minutes. Add the star fruit and lime juice to taste. Simmer for a further 2–3 minutes, until the fish is cooked.

**3** Make heaps of rice in four to six warmed bowls and use spoonfuls of the cooking liquid to moisten the rice.

**4** Divide the fish and star fruit between the bowls, spoon more of the cooking liquid over the top and garnish with basil leaves and a wedge of lime to squeeze over, if using.

SERVES FOUR TO SIX

INGREDIENTS
  30ml/2 tbsp coconut or palm oil
  about 900ml/1½ pints/3¾ cups
    water
  2 lemon grass stalks, bruised
  25g/1oz fresh root ginger,
    finely sliced
  about 700g/1lb 9oz freshwater or
    saltwater fish, such as trout or sea
    bream, cut into thin steaks
  2 firm star fruit (carambola), sliced
  juice of 1–2 limes

For the spice paste
  4 shallots, chopped
  4 fresh red chillies, seeded
    and chopped
  2 garlic cloves, chopped
  25g/1oz fresh galangal, chopped
  25g/1oz fresh turmeric,
    finely chopped
  3–4 candlenuts, chopped
To serve
  steamed rice
  1 bunch fresh basil leaves
    (optional)
  1 lime, cut into wedges (optional)

**Per Portion** Energy 240kcal/1001kJ; Protein 25.9g; Carbohydrate 7.3g, of which sugars 4.7g; Fat 12.1g, of which saturates 1.2g; Cholesterol 0mg; Calcium 27mg; Fibre 1.7g; Sodium 67mg.

# STUFFED CUCUMBERS WITH CRAB

*HERE, THE SIMPLE FRESHNESS OF THE CUCUMBER IS THE PERFECT FOIL TO THE RICH CRAB FILLING. THE DISH MAKES A PRETTY ADDITION TO A BUFFET TABLE BUT WORKS BEST AS A LIGHT AND ELEGANT APPETIZER, WITH HALF A CUCUMBER PER PERSON.*

SERVES EIGHT

INGREDIENTS
- 4 whole cucumbers
- 1 small carrot
- 300g/10½oz crab meat
- 2 spring onions (scallions), white parts only, finely chopped
- 30ml/2 tbsp sesame oil
- 15ml/1 tbsp fish sauce
- 1 egg, lightly beaten
- 15g/1 tbsp cornflour (cornstarch)

**4** Stuff each cucumber half with the crab mixture, patting it in well into the hollowed area.

**5** Place the cucumber halves in steamer baskets and steam over simmering water for 8 minutes until just done.

**1** Peel the cucumbers and cut each in half lengthways. Remove the seeds.

**2** Dice the carrot finely and boil in a little water for 3 minutes, then drain.

**3** Combine the crab meat with the spring onions, carrot, sesame oil, fish sauce, egg and cornflour. Mix well.

**COOK'S TIP**
Courgettes (zucchini) also make good 'boats' for this dish, and the crab meat can be replaced with prawns (shrimp) or minced (ground) pork, or even a combination of both.

**Per Portion** Energy 109kcal/453kJ; Protein 10g; Carbohydrate 3.9g, of which sugars 2g; Fat 6g, of which saturates 0.9g; Cholesterol 55mg; Calcium 22mg; Fibre 0.7g; Sodium 332mg.

# INDONESIAN YELLOW PRAWN CURRY

*COLOUR IS AN IMPORTANT PART OF INDONESIAN FOOD AND THE WORD UDANG, MEANING 'YELLOW', IS USED TO DESCRIBE THIS PRAWN DISH AS WELL AS THE POPULAR RICE DISH, NASI KUNING. BIG, JUICY PRAWNS ARE PARTICULARLY FAVOURED FOR THIS DISH IN BALI AND JAVA, BUT YOU CAN EASILY REPLACE THEM WITH SCALLOPS, SQUID OR MUSSELS, OR A COMBINATION OF ALL THREE.*

SERVES FOUR

INGREDIENTS
  30ml/2 tbsp coconut or palm oil
  2 shallots, finely chopped
  2 garlic cloves, finely chopped
  2 fresh red chillies, seeded and
    sliced lengthways
  25g/1oz fresh turmeric,
    finely chopped, or 10ml/2 tsp
    ground turmeric
  25g/1oz fresh root ginger,
    finely chopped
  2 lemon grass stalks,
    finely sliced
  10ml/2 tsp coriander seeds
  10ml/2 tsp terasi (Indonesian
    shrimp paste)
  1 red (bell) pepper, seeded and
    finely sliced
  4 kaffir lime leaves
  about 500g/1¼lb raw prawns
    (shrimp), shelled and deveined
  400g/14oz can coconut milk
  salt and ground black pepper
  cooked rice, to serve
To garnish
  4 fried shallots
  4 fresh green chillies, seeded and
    sliced diagonally

**1** Heat the oil in a wok or heavy pan, stir in the shallots, garlic, chillies, turmeric, ginger, lemon grass and coriander seeds and fry until fragrant.

**2** Stir in the terasi and cook the mixture for 2–3 minutes. Add the red pepper and kaffir lime leaves and stir-fry for 1 minute.

**3** Toss the prawns into the pan. Pour in the coconut milk and bring to the boil. Season the curry with salt and pepper to taste.

**4** Heap some cooked rice on to four warmed plates and spoon the prawn curry over the top.

**5** Garnish with fried shallots and sliced green chillies.

**COOK'S TIP**
For curries and adobo dishes that use a lot of prawns (shrimp), it is often more economical to buy frozen raw prawns at an Asian store rather than to obtain them fresh from the supermarket fish counter.

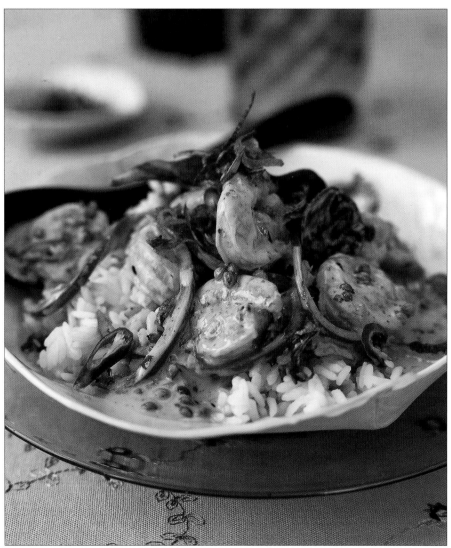

**Per Portion** Energy 230kcal/965kJ; Protein 26.4g; Carbohydrate 16g, of which sugars 13.5g; Fat 7.2g, of which saturates 1g; Cholesterol 263mg; Calcium 226mg; Fibre 2.7g; Sodium 519mg.

# SWEET AND SOUR PRAWNS

*INDONESIAN SWEET AND SOUR SAUCE DIFFERS FROM THE TRADITIONAL CHINESE VARIETY IN THAT IT IS A CLASSIC BLEND OF TOMATO KETCHUP, SOY SAUCE AND VINEGAR. THIS IS SIMPLE ENOUGH TO MAKE AT HOME, AS THIS RECIPE SHOWS, BUT YOU CAN ALSO USE ANY STORE-BOUGHT VARIETY THAT YOU LIKE FOR SPEED AND CONVENIENCE, AS THEY ARE JUST AS TASTY TOO.*

SERVES FOUR

INGREDIENTS
    16 raw tiger prawns (jumbo shrimp)
    30ml/2 tbsp cornflour (cornstarch)
    1 egg, lightly beaten
    vegetable oil for deep-frying
For the sweet and sour sauce
    15ml/1 tbsp light soy sauce
    45g/3 tbsp tomato ketchup
    30ml/2 tbsp vinegar
    15ml/1 tbsp sugar
    100ml/3½fl oz/⅓ cup water
    5ml/1 tsp cornflour (cornstarch)

**1** Shell the prawns, removing the heads but leaving the tails intact.

**2** Dredge the prawns with the cornflour, then dip them in the egg. Heat enough oil for deep-frying, then deep-fry the prawns in batches until crisp and golden brown. Set aside to keep warm.

**3** Blend all the sauce ingredients except for the cornflour and bring to the boil in a small pan.

**4** Blend the cornflour with a little water and add to the sauce, stirring to prevent any lumps forming.

**5** Cook the sauce, stirring, for 1 minute until thickened. Place the prawns in four bowls and pour over the sauce.

**Per Portion** Energy 224kcal/933kJ; Protein 10.1g; Carbohydrate 16.9g, of which sugars 0.5g; Fat 12.9g, of which saturates 1.7g; Cholesterol 78mg; Calcium 62mg; Fibre 0.3g; Sodium 256mg.

# POULTRY

*After sampling some of the delicious treatments given to chicken, duck and other poultry by Indonesians, you may be reluctant to return to traditional Western cooking methods. With fragrant and meltingly tender stews, irresistibly crunchy deep-fried dishes, deliciously different roasts and spicy stuffings, this chapter is full of inspiration.*

# Spicy Chicken Parcels

*Tum ayam is popular in Indonesia as an appetizer. Tum means cooking spiced foods wrapped in banana leaves. The method can be applied to a whole range of ingredients such as fish cutlets, prawns (shrimp), pork, beef and duck. Minced chicken is particularly good as it absorbs the spice mix effectively and cooks quickly.*

SERVES FOUR

INGREDIENTS

- 450g/1lb minced (ground) chicken
- 30ml/2 tbsp Shallot and Lemon Grass Sambal (see page 18)
- 1 egg, lightly beaten
- 105ml/7 tbsp coconut milk
- 5 salam leaves (Indonesian bay leaves), finely shredded
- 4 lime leaves, finely shredded
- 2.5ml/½ tsp salt
- 2.5ml/½ tsp sugar
- juice of 1 lime
- 10 pieces of banana leaf, each measuring 20cm/8in square

**1** Combine all the ingredients except for the banana leaves and mix well.

**2** Blanch the banana leaves in boiling water to make them more pliable.

**3** Divide the chicken mixture between the banana leaves and wrap up to make 10 parcels.

**4** Secure each parcel with cocktail sticks (toothpicks) and place them in a steamer. Cook for 20 minutes and serve warm as an appetizer, either still wrapped in the leaves or unwrapped. Do not eat the banana leaves.

**Per Portion** Energy 148kcal/622kJ; Protein 28.7g; Carbohydrate 1.1g, of which sugars 1g; Fat 3.2g, of which saturates 0.8g; Cholesterol 127mg; Calcium 16mg; Fibre 0.1g; Sodium 109mg.

# INDONESIAN FRIED CHICKEN

*THIS SPICY DISH PUTS WESTERN FRIED CHICKEN TO SHAME. FIRST OF ALL THE CHICKEN IS COOKED IN SPICE PASTE TO ENSURE A DEPTH OF FLAVOUR AND THEN IT IS SIMPLY DEEP-FRIED TO FORM A CRISP, GOLDEN SKIN. SERVE WITH A SAMBAL OR PICKLE FOR A DELICIOUS SNACK OR, FOR A TASTY MEAL, ACCOMPANY IT WITH YELLOW OR FRAGRANT COCONUT RICE AND A SALAD.*

SERVES FOUR

INGREDIENTS
　12 chicken thighs or drumsticks,
　　or 12 legs, separated into thighs
　　and drumsticks
　30ml/2 tbsp kecap manis (Indonesian
　　sweet soy sauce)
　150ml/¼ pint/⅔ cup water
　vegetable oil, for deep-frying
　salt and ground black pepper
　sambal or pickle, to serve
For the spice paste
　2 shallots, chopped
　4 garlic cloves, chopped
　50g/2oz fresh root ginger, chopped
　25g/1oz fresh turmeric, chopped
　2 lemon grass stalks, chopped

**1** Grind the spice paste ingredients to a coarse paste using a mortar and pestle or an electric food processor or blender.

**2** Put the chicken pieces in a large, flameproof casserole or heavy pan and smear the spice paste over them.

**3** Add the kecap manis and the water to the pan and bring to the boil, then reduce the heat and simmer, uncovered, for about 25 minutes.

**4** Turn the chicken occasionally, until all the liquid has evaporated. You need the chicken to be dry before you deep-fry it, but the spices should be sticking to it. Season the chicken pieces with salt and pepper.

**5** Heat enough oil for deep-frying in a wok. Add the chicken pieces, in batches, and fry for 6–8 minutes until golden brown and crisp. Remove from the wok with a slotted spoon, drain on kitchen paper and serve hot.

**COOK'S TIP**
Kecap manis is soy sauce sweetened with palm sugar (jaggery). If you cannot find it, replace it with the same quantity of dark soy sauce and 15ml/1 tbsp sugar.

**Per Portion** Energy 410kcal/1719kJ; Protein 60.8g; Carbohydrate 4.6g, of which sugars 3.4g; Fat 16.6g, of which saturates 2.4g; Cholesterol 175mg; Calcium 26mg; Fibre 0.7g; Sodium 686mg.

# INDONESIAN CHICKEN AND PRAWN SALAD

*SPICY AND REFRESHING CHICKEN AND/OR SHELLFISH SALADS ARE POPULAR AT INDONESIAN FOOD STALLS AND AS PART OF LARGE, CELEBRATORY FEASTS. THIS DISH IS A REAL CLASSIC, WITH TENDER STRIPS OF CHICKEN AND MEATY PRAWNS IRRESISTIBLY FLAVOURED WITH THE SWEET, GINGERY HEAT OF GALANGAL, COLOURED WITH GOLDEN TURMERIC AND TOSSED IN A FRESH, ZESTY TOMATO SAUCE.*

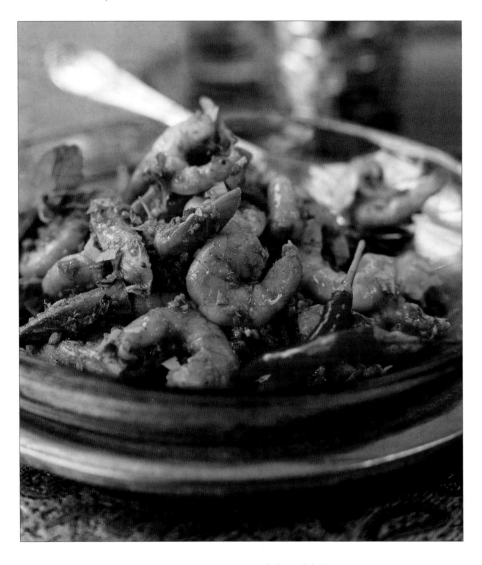

**1** Cook the chicken pieces by steaming, roasting or boiling. When cooked, if using chicken breast fillets, cut the meat into thin strips; if using thighs, shred the meat with your fingers.

**2** Boil or steam the prawns for 2–3 minutes, until opaque. Drain, refresh in cold water and drain again. Put aside.

**3** To make the spice paste, grind the shallots, garlic, chillies, galangal, turmeric, lemon grass and candlenuts together using a mortar and pestle.

**4** Heat the oil in a heavy pan, stir in the spice paste and fry until fragrant. Add the terasi and palm sugar and stir for 3–4 minutes, until the paste starts to brown. Add the tomatoes, coriander, mint and lime juice and cook for 5–10 minutes, until the sauce is reduced and thick. Season to taste and leave to cool.

**5** Add the chicken and prawns to the sauce and toss together. Transfer to a dish and serve with lime wedges to squeeze over, and chillies to chew on.

SERVES FOUR

INGREDIENTS
500g/1¼lb chicken breast fillets
  or thighs
225g/8oz prawns (shrimp), peeled
  and deveined
30ml/2 tbsp groundnut (peanut) oil
5ml/1 tsp terasi (Indonesian
  shrimp paste)
10ml/2 tsp palm sugar (jaggery)
2 tomatoes, skinned, seeded
  and chopped
1 bunch fresh coriander (cilantro)
  leaves, chopped
1 bunch fresh mint leaves, chopped
juice of 1 lime
salt and ground black pepper
For the spice paste
  2 shallots, chopped
  2 garlic cloves, chopped
  2–3 fresh red chillies, seeded
    and chopped
  25g/1oz fresh galangal, chopped
  15g/½ oz fresh turmeric, chopped,
    or 2.5ml/½ tsp ground turmeric
  1 lemon grass stalk, chopped
  2 candlenuts, chopped
To serve
  1 lime, quartered (optional)
  2 green or red chillies, seeded and
    cut into quarters lengthways

**Per Portion** Energy 274kcal/1154kJ; Protein 41.6g; Carbohydrate 10.4g, of which sugars 8.7g; Fat 7.7g, of which saturates 1.1g; Cholesterol 197mg; Calcium 99mg; Fibre 2.2g; Sodium 193mg.

# SHREDDED CHICKEN

*ABON DESCRIBES MEATS THAT HAVE BEEN COOKED AND FLAKED. THIS DISH, AYAM ABON ABON, IS NOT DIFFICULT TO MAKE AT HOME ALTHOUGH IT IS SOLD READY-MADE THROUGHOUT INDONESIA. IT IS OFTEN MADE WITH BEEF AND OCCASIONALLY FISH, WHILE INDONESIAN CHINESE GENERALLY USE PORK, BUT THIS VERSION USES CHICKEN, WHICH IS EASIER TO SHRED.*

SERVES FOUR

INGREDIENTS
    1 chicken, about 600g/1lb 6oz
    5ml/1 tsp ground coriander
    2 slices galangal
    5ml/1 tsp garlic purée (paste)
    2.5ml/½ tsp salt
    60ml/4 tbsp vegetable oil
    shredded cucumber and lettuce

**3** Once the strained chicken has cooled, use your hands or a sharp knife, flake or slice the chicken into thin strips, removing the skin if you prefer to have a healthier dish.

**4** Mix the chicken with the coriander, galangal, garlic and salt. Heat the oil in a large wok and fry the chicken over a high heat until crisp. Serve as a salad on a bed of shredded cucumber and lettuce.

**1** Put the chicken in a large pan and just cover it in water. Bring to the boil, then simmer for 35 minutes. Strain and cool, reserving the stock if you wish.

**2** Dry-fry the ground coriander over a low–moderate heat until fragrant. Grate the galangal finely.

**COOK'S TIPS**
• Use skinless chicken breast fillets for a less fatty dish that also saves some time and effort.
• Make your own garlic purée by pulping peeled garlic cloves in a mortar and pestle or rubbing them through a fine grater.

Per Portion Energy 324kcal/1342kJ; Protein 19.3g; Carbohydrate 2.1g, of which sugars 0.2g; Fat 26.5g, of which saturates 5.8g; Cholesterol 96mg; Calcium 10mg; Fibre 0.5g; Sodium 76mg.

# CHICKEN IN WHITE COCONUT MILK SAUCE

*OPOR DISHES ARE AMONG THE MILDEST OF INDONESIAN RECIPES, OPOR BEING A NAME GIVEN TO NON-CHILLI-BASED CURRIES. THIS MILD, CREAMY STEW MAKES A GOOD INTRODUCTION TO CURRIES FOR THOSE PEOPLE WHO ARE NOT ACCUSTOMED TO CHILLI FIRE. IT IS DELICIOUS SERVED WITH CHUNKS OF CRUSTY BAGUETTE OR WITH PLAIN BOILED RICE.*

**2** Add the chicken pieces and lemon grass to the pan and continue to fry for 5 minutes, stirring frequently.

**3** Transfer to a heavy pan and add the salam leaves, coconut milk and salt. Bring to the boil, then reduce the heat and simmer, covered, for 35 minutes.

**4** Serve the dish in warmed bowls, garnished with the reserved fried garlic and shallots, with rice and lime slices.

### SERVES FOUR

INGREDIENTS
    30ml/2 tbsp vegetable oil
    8 shallots, sliced
    7 garlic cloves, sliced
    15ml/1 tbsp ground coriander
    5ml/1 tsp chopped fresh root ginger
    1 chicken, about 600g/1lb 6oz, cut
      into 5cm/2in pieces on the bone
    2 lemon grass stalks, 5cm/2in of root
      end bruised
    4 salam leaves (Indonesian bay leaves)
    450ml/¾ pint/scant 2 cups
      coconut milk
    5ml/1 tsp salt
    lime slices, to garnish
    boiled rice, to serve

**1** Heat the oil in a wok and fry the shallots and garlic until light golden. Remove three-quarters of the shallots and half the garlic from the pan and set aside to use as a garnish. Add the ground coriander and chopped ginger and fry for 2 minutes.

**COOK'S TIP**
If you want to add a little fire, slit 2 or 3 green chillies lengthways but not all the way through. Seed them and add in the last 10 minutes of cooking.

**Per Portion** Energy 311kcal/1294kJ; Protein 19.8g; Carbohydrate 9.3g, of which sugars 6.9g; Fat 22g, of which saturates 5.5g; Cholesterol 96mg; Calcium 56mg; Fibre 0.4g; Sodium 202mg.

# TANGY CHICKEN STEW

*THIS SIMPLE BUT VERY FLAVOURSOME CASSEROLED CHICKEN MAY WELL BECOME ONE OF YOUR FAVOURITE 'EVERYDAY' DISHES. THE TENDER CHICKEN PIECES ARE COATED IN A TANGY, ALMOST SWEET AND SOUR SAUCE THAT IS VERY EASY TO MAKE AND HAS A PLEASANT KICK OF HEAT. THE DISH TASTES WONDERFUL SERVED WITH PLAIN JASMINE RICE AND SOME STEAMED GREEN VEGETABLES.*

SERVES FOUR

INGREDIENTS

- 4 whole chicken legs
- 2.5ml/½ tsp salt
- 2.5ml/½ tsp black peppercorns
- 4 garlic cloves, chopped
- 2 bay leaves
- 75ml/2½fl oz/½ cup coconut vinegar
- 10ml/2 tsp chilli powder
- 200ml/7fl oz/1 cup water
- 6 shallots, sliced
- 2 tomatoes, chopped
- boiled rice, to serve

**3** Add the water, shallots and tomatoes and cook over a high heat until the sauce has reduced by half. Taste and adjust the seasoning as desired, then serve the chicken hot with rice.

**1** Use a heavy knife to divide each chicken leg into three pieces, removing and discarding any excess skin and fat to leave lean portions.

**2** Place the chicken in a pan with the salt, peppercorns, garlic, bay leaves and coconut vinegar. Bring to the boil, reduce the heat and simmer very gently for 15 minutes, turning the meat occasionally, until nearly all the liquid has evaporated. Add the chilli powder and continue cooking for 5 minutes.

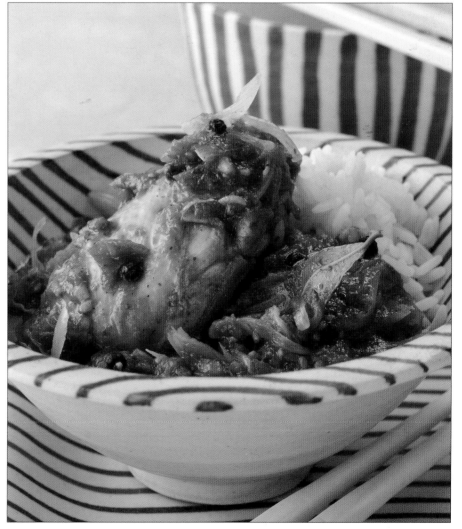

**Per Portion** Energy 221kcal/922kJ; Protein 19.8g; Carbohydrate 3.6g, of which sugars 2.4g; Fat 14.3g, of which saturates 3.9g; Cholesterol 116mg; Calcium 19mg; Fibre 0.7g; Sodium 88mg.

# BALI FRIED POUSSINS

*In Bali, siap megoreng is practically a national dish and is offered in reverence to deities during religious festivals. It is usually grilled or barbecued, although it can also be pan-fried, the latter method being easier unless you are using the barbecue anyway. Poussins are best for this dish as they are more tender and cook more quickly than chicken.*

## SERVES 4

### INGREDIENTS

4 poussins
150g/5oz Balinese Spice Paste
  (see page 18)
450ml/14fl oz/1⅔ cups
  coconut milk
3 lemon grass stalks, 5cm/2in
  of root end bruised
5 salam leaves (Indonesian bay leaves)
5ml/1 tsp salt
5ml/1 tsp black peppercorns, crushed
105ml/7 tbsp vegetable oil
juice of 1 lime
4 limes, halved, to garnish
chilli dipping sauce, to serve

**1** Spatchcock each poussin by cutting down the backbone and spreading out the bird so that the breast is one broad piece and the bird lies flat on the work surface. Alternatively, ask your butcher to do this for you.

**2** Whisk together the spice paste and coconut milk, and bring to the boil with the lemon grass, salam leaves, salt and peppercorns. Simmer the poussins in this blend for 8 minutes. If your pot is too crowded, cook in two batches.

**3** Remove the poussins and drain. Heat the oil in a large wok or frying pan and fry the poussins, two at a time, until the skin is golden brown. Turn once or twice to make sure they cook thoroughly.

**4** In the last few minutes of cooking, drizzle the lime juice over the poussins, and serve warm with a chilli dipping sauce and lime halves to squeeze over.

**Per Portion** Energy 288kcal/1200kJ; Protein 24.3g; Carbohydrate 3.5g, of which sugars 2.9g; Fat 20.6g, of which saturates 4.9g; Cholesterol 123mg; Calcium 47mg; Fibre 0.5g; Sodium 183mg.

# MARINATED DUCK

*IN INDONESIA, DUCK IS CALLED DIFFERENT NAMES ACCORDING TO LOCAL DIALECT. IT COULD BE BEBEK, ENTOK OR ITIK, DEPENDING ON WHERE YOU ARE. THIS RECIPE IS IDEAL FOR THE READILY-AVAILABLE BARBARY DUCK BREASTS. ROASTING THEM OVER WATER KEEPS THE FLESH MOIST AND TENDER, AND THE INFUSION OF GINGER AND SPICE IS TRULY HEAVENLY.*

**SERVES TWO**

INGREDIENTS
    breasts of one large duck, trimmed
        of fat and excess skin
To serve
    baby spinach leaves and cucumber
    sweet chilli dip
For the spice paste
    3 fresh green chillies, seeded
        and chopped
    4 shallots, chopped
    4 garlic cloves, chopped
    2 candlenuts, chopped
    5ml/1 tsp grated fresh
        root ginger
    1 lemon grass stalk, 5cm/2in
        of root end chopped
    6 green peppercorns
    juice of 3 limes
    30ml/2 tbsp tamarind concentrate
    1.5ml/¼ tsp salt
    5ml/1 tsp sugar
    120ml/4fl oz/½ cup water

**1** Grind the chillies, shallots, garlic, candlenuts, ginger, lemon grass and peppercorns to a fine paste with a mortar and pestle or blender. Combine with the lime juice, tamarind, salt, sugar and water in a small pan, and cook over a low heat until a thick sauce forms.

**COOK'S TIPS**
• These duck breasts are also excellent as a barbecue item. Cook on charcoal until the skins just begin to char.
• If you can't buy duck breasts, cut the breasts from a whole duck.

**2** Allow to cool, then smear all over the duck breasts and marinate in the refrigerator for a few hours or overnight.

**3** Preheat the oven to 200°C/400°F/ Gas 6. Place the duck on a rack in a baking tray and brush with marinade.

**4** Half fill the baking tray with water. Roast the duck for 30 minutes, leave to cool, then slice.

**5** Serve with baby spinach leaves and sliced cucumber, with a sweet chilli dip on the side.

**Per Portion** Energy 249kcal/1045kJ; Protein 32.5g; Carbohydrate 7.3g, of which sugars 4.3g; Fat 12.8g, of which saturates 2.2g; Cholesterol 165mg; Calcium 45mg; Fibre 1.4g; Sodium 660mg.

# BALINESE SMOKED DUCK

*In the villages of Indonesia, this dish of slow-cooked, tender duck is prepared for feasts. Smeared with spices and herbs and tightly wrapped in banana or pandanus leaves, the duck is smoked in the embers of a fire made from coconut husks until the aromatic meat is so tender that it falls off the bone. This version is cooked in the oven.*

SERVES FOUR

INGREDIENTS

1.8kg/4lb oven-ready duck
1 large banana leaf or aluminium foil
salt and ground black pepper

For the spice paste

6–8 shallots, chopped
4 garlic cloves, chopped
4 fresh chillies, seeded and chopped
25g/1oz fresh root ginger, chopped
50g/2oz fresh turmeric, chopped,
  or 25ml/1½ tbsp ground turmeric
2 lemon grass stalks, chopped
4 lime leaves, crumbled
4 candlenuts, chopped
10ml/2 tsp coriander seeds
15ml/1 tbsp terasi (Indonesian
  shrimp paste)
15–30ml/1–2 tbsp water

**1** First make the spice paste. Using a mortar and pestle or a blender, grind all the ingredients except the terasi and water together to form a smooth paste. Add the terasi and water and mix together until the mixture becomes a thick paste.

**2** Preheat the oven to 160°C/325°F/ Gas 3. Rub the spice paste all over the duck, inside and out, and sprinkle with salt and pepper. Place the duck in the centre of the banana leaf or a sheet of foil. If using a banana leaf, secure it with string. If using foil, tuck in the short sides and fold the long sides over the top to form a parcel. Place the parcel in a roasting pan.

**3** Roast the duck for 4–5 hours, then open the parcel to reveal the top of the duck and roast for a further 30–45 minutes to brown the skin. Serve immediately.

**Per Portion** Energy 234kcal/982kJ; Protein 26.9g; Carbohydrate 12.8g, of which sugars 8.4g; Fat 8.8g, of which saturates 2.7g; Cholesterol 135mg; Calcium 75mg; Fibre 3g; Sodium 161mg.

# SUMATRAN DUCK WITH CHILLIES

*This unusual duck recipe makes the most of the natural affinity between the rich duck flesh and sweet, spicy flavours. The chillies give a gently pleasing, but not overpowering, heat, while the lemon grass and lime leaves add an irresistible tanginess and aroma. The dish is best enjoyed with steamed jasmine rice and tender seasonal vegetables.*

SERVES SIX TO EIGHT

INGREDIENTS
    1 oven-ready duck
    45ml/3 tbsp vegetable oil
    750ml/1¼ pints/3 cups water
    30ml/2 tbsp tamarind concentrate
    1.5ml/¼ tsp salt
    5ml/1 tsp sugar
    2 lemon grass stalks, 5cm/2in of
      root end bruised
    4 fresh green chillies, seeded
For the spice paste
    5 fresh green chillies, seeded
      and chopped
    1 large onion, chopped
    6 candlenuts, chopped
    30ml/2 tbsp ground ginger
    15g/1 tbsp galangal
    2 lemon grass stalks, 5cm/2in of
      root end chopped
    1.5ml/¼ tsp ground turmeric
    4 lime leaves, spines removed
    2.5ml/½ tsp black peppercorns

**1** Chop the whole duck into about 8–10 pieces, removing any excess fat and the skin.

**2** Process or pound the spice paste ingredients in a mortar and pestle to form a fine paste. Heat the oil and fry the paste over a low heat for 5 minutes.

**COOK'S TIPS**
• For a milder tasting dish, simply reduce the number of chillies.
• Serve with a dollop of crème fraîche on the side for a creamier taste and texture.

**3** Transfer the paste to a large pot and combine with the duck, water, tamarind, salt, sugar and lemon grass. Bring to the boil, then reduce the heat and simmer for 1 hour. The sauce should reduce by half. Slice and add the chillies in the last 5 minutes of cooking. Serve hot with steamed rice and vegetables.

Per Portion Energy 137kcal/573kJ; Protein 14.5g; Carbohydrate 0.2g, of which sugars 0.2g; Fat 8.8g, of which saturates 2g; Cholesterol 75mg; Calcium 15mg; Fibre 0g; Sodium 79mg.

# MEAT

Visitors to Indonesia will most often encounter meat
dishes of pork, beef or lamb, but it is also common to eat
buffalo and goat. Using their own distinctive local
flavourings, such as coconut, spices, tomatoes or vinegar,
Indonesian cooks like to simmer meat slowly in delicious
broths and sauces to make rich stews and curries.

# HOT LAMB CURRY

*PARSANGA IS AN EXTREMELY AROMATIC AND SPICY DRY CURRY BLENDED WITH FRIED COCONUT, ALMOST LIKE A RENDANG. LAMB IS THE USUAL MEAT, ALTHOUGH THERE IS NO REASON WHY YOU CANNOT CHOOSE PORK OR CHICKEN INSTEAD. IT IS FAIRLY COMPLEX IN PREPARATION BUT THE ACTUAL COOKING IS NOTHING MORE THAN LONG SIMMERING.*

SERVES FOUR

INGREDIENTS

150g/5oz desiccated (dry
  unsweetened shredded) coconut
900g/1kg lean lamb
small piece of nutmeg, chopped
3 cloves
2 cardamoms
2 lemon grass stalks, 5cm/2in of
  root end bruised
1 litre/1¾ pints/4 cups coconut milk
1 tsp salt
boiled rice, to serve

**COOK'S TIP**
For a quick dish, you can use curry
powder instead of making the spice
paste, but add a few slices of galangal.

For the spice paste
30ml/2 tbsp ground coriander
10ml/2 tsp black peppercorns
5ml/1 tsp ground cumin
5 fresh red chillies, seeded
  and chopped
4 garlic cloves
30g/2 tbsp grated fresh
  root ginger
15ml/1 tbsp grated fresh galangal
To garnish
fresh red chillies, sliced diagonally
coriander (cilantro) leaves

**1** Place all the spice paste ingredients
in a mortar and pestle or a food
processor, and blend or process to a
coarse paste. Add a little water to
thicken the paste.

**2** Dry-fry the coconut over a low heat
for 10 minutes until golden brown,
then process in a blender or mortar and
pestle until fine.

**3** Combine all the ingredients in a pan
and bring to the boil. Cook for 20 minutes
on high, then turn the heat down to
medium to simmer for 1 hour or more,
until the liquid is thick and oily.

**4** Spoon off any excess oil and discard.
Garnish the lamb with chillies and
coriander and serve with rice.

Per Portion Energy 723kcal/3017kJ; Protein 49.2g; Carbohydrate 19.1g, of which sugars 14.8g; Fat 50.9g, of which saturates 32.5g; Cholesterol 171mg; Calcium 126mg; Fibre 5.2g; Sodium 484mg.

# MUTTON KORMA

*KORMA IS RESOLUTELY OF INDIAN ORIGIN AND A STAPLE OF THE MUSLIM COMMUNITY IN THE SUB-CONTINENT. IT IS THE GENERAL BELIEF THAT IT CAME FROM THE MUGHAL RULERS, WHO LIKED THEIR SPICED DISHES CREAMY. INDONESIA WAS PART OF THE ANCIENT HINDU KINGDOM OF SRI VIJAYA AND THIS DISH REMAINS A FIRM FAVOURITE OF THE REGION.*

### SERVES FOUR

INGREDIENTS
- 900g/1kg mutton, cut into bitesize chunks
- 45ml/3 tbsp ghee
- 1 large onion, sliced
- 4 garlic cloves, chopped
- 2 lemon grass stalks, 5cm/2in of root end chopped
- 1 x 5cm/2in cinnamon stick
- 4 salam leaves (Indonesian bay leaves)
- 600ml/1 pint/2½ cups water
- 200ml/7fl oz/¾ cup coconut milk
- 105ml/7 tbsp natural (plain) yogurt
- 10ml/2 tsp salt
- 5ml/1 tsp sugar
- 450g/1lb potatoes, cut into bitesize chunks
- cooked rice, to serve

For the spice paste
- 4 cardamoms
- 4 cloves
- 12 black peppercorns
- 30g/2 tbsp ground coriander
- 5ml/1 tsp ground cumin
- 5ml/1 tsp ground fennel seeds

**1** Grind the cardamoms, cloves and peppercorns with a mortar and pestle until very fine.

**2** Mix in the ground coriander, cumin and fennel. Add a little water to make a fairly thick paste.

**3** Coat the chunks of mutton well with the spice paste. Leave to marinate for about 20 minutes.

**4** Heat the ghee in a large pan or wok and fry the onion and garlic for 2 minutes until soft. Add the mutton and stir-fry for 5 minutes. Add the lemon grass, cinnamon, salam leaves and water, bring to the boil, then simmer for 30 minutes.

**5** Add the coconut milk, yogurt, salt, sugar and potatoes to the pan, return to the boil, then continue to simmer, covered, for another 30 minutes until the mutton is tender. Serve the mutton curry with rice.

**Per Portion** Energy 679kcal/2838kJ; Protein 50.1g; Carbohydrate 36.1g, of which sugars 13.9g; Fat 38.4g, of which saturates 19.6g; Cholesterol 203mg; Calcium 135mg; Fibre 2.9g; Sodium 1272mg.

# BRAISED MUTTON IN KECAP MANIS

*SMOOR, OR SEMUR, IS THE NAME FOR DISHES COOKED IN DARK SOY SAUCE AND TOUCHED WITH SUGAR AND TAMARIND. IT IS BELIEVED TO HAVE ORIGINATED IN JAVA, WHERE KECAP MANIS (SWEET SOY SAUCE) IS A PRIMARY INGREDIENT. IT IS A DISH THAT REFLECTS BOTH CHINESE AND INDIGENOUS INDONESIAN ELEMENTS: SOY SAUCE AND THE HEADY SCENT OF NUTMEG, CINNAMON, CLOVES AND STAR ANISE.*

**2** Heat the oil in a wok or frying pan and fry the onion for 2 minutes until soft. Add the meat and all other ingredients, and stir-fry over medium heat for 2 minutes.

**3** Top up with about 400ml/14fl oz/1⅔ cups of the reserved stock, and cook, uncovered, over a high heat until the sauce is well reduced and thick, lowering the heat if the reduction is too rapid. This will take approximately 30 minutes, depending on your pan: the evaporation rate in a deep pan is slower than in a wider wok or frying pan. Adjust the seasoning and serve.

SERVES FOUR

INGREDIENTS
    600g/1lb 6oz lean mutton or lamb
    30ml/2 tbsp vegetable oil
    1 large onion, sliced
    pinch of ground nutmeg
    6 cloves
    1 cinnamon stick, about
        4cm/1½in long
    1 star anise
    2.5ml/½ tsp black peppercorns
    45ml/3 tbsp kecap manis (Indonesian
        sweet soy sauce)
    15ml/1 tbsp tamarind concentrate
    2.5ml/½ tsp salt

**1** Boil the mutton or lamb in a large pot of water for 45 minutes or until tender. Strain, reserving the liquid. Cut the meat into thin slices or small chunks, as you prefer.

**Per Portion** Energy 373kcal/1554kJ; Protein 31.7g; Carbohydrate 10.5g, of which sugars 6.3g; Fat 23.2g, of which saturates 8.5g; Cholesterol 114mg; Calcium 48mg; Fibre 1.4g; Sodium 846mg.

# BRAISED PORK <u>IN</u> TOMATO SAUCE

*ALSO CALLED FRITTATA, THIS IS OF SPANISH ORIGIN AND REFERS TO DISHES COOKED WITH TOMATOES, GARLIC AND OLIVE OIL. FRITTATA MEANS FRIED IN SPANISH AND THE DISTINCTIVE FLAVOUR COMES FROM SAUTÉED MEAT OR CHICKEN SIMMERED WITH TOMATOES AND BULKED UP WITH POTATOES AND ONIONS. IN SOME REGIONS, JALAPEÑO CHILLIES ARE ADDED. THIS TASTES EVEN BETTER THE DAY AFTER COOKING.*

### SERVES FOUR

INGREDIENTS

450g/1lb leg of pork, trimmed and cut into 2.5cm/1in cubes
2.5ml/½ tsp salt
2.5ml/½ tsp ground black pepper
30ml/2 tbsp olive oil
105ml/7 tbsp water
1 large Spanish onion, thinly sliced
3 garlic cloves, finely chopped
2 large beef tomatoes, sliced
105ml/7 tbsp tomato ketchup
300g/11oz potatoes, diced
2 jalapeño chillies (optional)
1 red (bell) pepper, seeded and sliced into strips
15ml/1 tbsp fish sauce
coriander (cilantro) leaves, to garnish

**3** Add the water, onion, garlic, tomatoes, tomato ketchup, potatoes and jalapeños, if using, and simmer for 30 minutes.

**4** Add the pepper to the pan with the fish sauce. Simmer for another 15 minutes and serve garnished with coriander.

**1** Sprinkle the cubed pork with salt and pepper. Set aside at room temperature for 15 minutes.

**2** Heat the olive oil in a wok or heavy frying pan and stir-fry the seasoned pork until it is well sizzled and light brown all over.

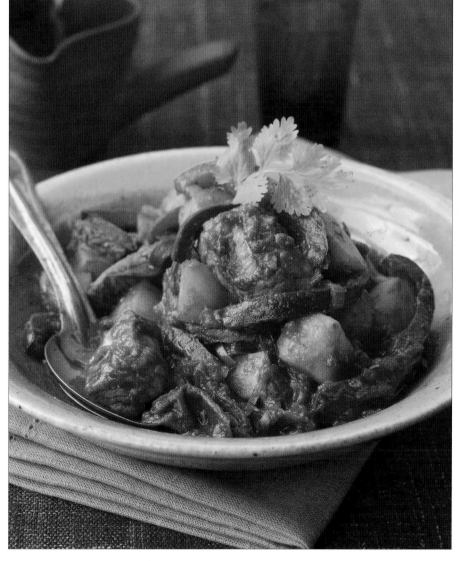

**Per Portion** Energy 328kcal/1376kJ; Protein 27.8g; Carbohydrate 31.8g, of which sugars 18g; Fat 10.8g, of which saturates 2.4g; Cholesterol 71mg; Calcium 48mg; Fibre 3.6g; Sodium 524mg.

# SLOW-COOKED BUFFALO IN COCONUT MILK

*THIS IS ONE OF INDONESIA'S MOST POPULAR AND BEST-KNOWN MEAT DISHES. TRADITIONALLY MADE WITH THE MEAT OF WATER BUFFALO, ALTHOUGH PRIME BEEF IS EQUALLY DELICIOUS, THE DISH IS COOKED SLOWLY TO ACHIEVE THE REQUIRED TENDERNESS AND TO CREATE A RICH SAUCE.*

SERVES SIX

INGREDIENTS

1kg/2¼lb buffalo or beef, such as
   topside (pot roast) or rump (round)
   steak, cut into bitesize cubes
15ml/1 tbsp tamarind paste
90ml/6 tbsp water
115g/4oz fresh coconut, grated,
   or desiccated (dry unsweetened
   shredded) coconut
45ml/3 tbsp coconut, corn or
   groundnut (peanut) oil
2 onions, sliced
3 lemon grass stalks, halved
   and bruised
2 cinnamon sticks
3–4 lime leaves
1.2 litres/2 pints/5 cups
   coconut milk
15ml/1 tbsp sugar
salt and ground black pepper

For the spice paste
   8–10 dried red chillies
   8 shallots, chopped
   4–6 garlic cloves, chopped
   50g/2oz fresh galangal, chopped
   25g/1oz fresh turmeric, chopped
   15ml/1 tbsp coriander seeds
   10ml/2 tsp cumin seeds
   5ml/1 tsp black peppercorns
To serve
   6–8 shallots, sliced
   cooked rice
   a salad (optional)

1 For the spice paste, soak the chillies in warm water for 30 minutes. Drain, remove the seeds, then squeeze dry.

2 With a mortar and pestle or a food processor, grind the chillies, shallots, garlic, galangal and turmeric to a smooth paste.

3 In a heavy pan, dry-fry the coriander, cumin seeds and peppercorns for a few minutes. Grind to a powder, then stir into the spice paste.

4 Put the buffalo or beef in a large bowl, add the spice paste and mix together until coated. Leave to marinate, at room temperature or in the refrigerator, for at least 2 hours if using buffalo or 1 hour if using beef.

5 Meanwhile, put the tamarind paste and water in a bowl and leave to soak for about 30 minutes until soft. Using a heavy frying pan, dry-fry the grated coconut until it is brown and gives off a nutty aroma. Using a mortar and pestle, or a food processor, grind the dry-fried coconut until it resembles brown sugar. Set aside. Squeeze the tamarind to help soften it and then strain to extract the juice. Discard the pulp.

6 Heat the oil in a wok with a lid or large, heavy pan. Add the onions, lemon grass, cinnamon sticks and lime leaves, and fry for 5–10 minutes until the onions begin to colour.

7 Add the beef with all the spice paste and stir-fry until lightly browned. Add the coconut milk and tamarind juice and bring to the boil, stirring all the time. Reduce the heat and simmer gently for 4 hours for buffalo (2–4 hours for beef) until the sauce begins to thicken.

8 Stir in the sugar and ground coconut, cover and simmer very gently for another 4 hours for buffalo and 2–4 hours for beef, stirring occasionally, until the meat is tender and the sauce is thick.

9 Meanwhile, fry the sliced shallots in the corn oil until golden, then drain.

10 When the meat is tender, season to taste and spoon it on to a serving dish. Sprinkle the fried shallots over the top and serve with rice and a salad.

**Per Portion** Energy 494kcal/2064kJ; Protein 40.6g; Carbohydrate 20.9g, of which sugars 18.8g; Fat 28.2g, of which saturates 17g; Cholesterol 97mg; Calcium 95mg; Fibre 3.9g; Sodium 335mg.

# TAMARIND PICKLED BEEF

*IN MANY PARTS OF INDONESIA, BEEF HAS TRADITIONALLY COME FROM WATER BUFFALO. THESE DAYS, HOWEVER, WITH IMPORTED MEAT FROM NEARBY COUNTRIES SUCH AS AUSTRALIA AND NEW ZEALAND, THE INDONESIANS USE THE SAME KIND OF BEEF THAT YOU WOULD FIND IN ANY SUPERMARKET.*

SERVES FOUR

INGREDIENTS
    450g/1lb stewing steak
    500ml/17fl oz/2 cups water
    25g/1oz galangal
    45ml/3 tbsp oil
    5ml/1 tsp salt
    5ml/1 tsp sugar
    5ml/1 tsp ground black pepper
    30ml/2 tbsp tamarind concentrate
    prawn crackers, to serve

**1** Cut the beef into finger-length pieces, about 1.5cm/½in thick.

**2** Put the beef pieces in a wok or pan with the water and bring to the boil. Cook until almost dry. This should take about 20–25 minutes in a wok.

**3** Grind the galangal with a mortar and pestle until fine.

**4** Heat the oil in a wok and fry the galangal for 1 minute. Add the boiled beef, salt, sugar and pepper, and stir-fry over a medium heat until the flavours are well incorporated – about 1 minute.

**5** Add the tamarind concentrate and continue to fry until nearly dry and the beef is fork tender.

**6** Serve as part of a main meal, or as finger food with some prawn crackers.

**VARIATION**
If you prefer to use sirloin or rump steak, reduce the water by one third.

**Per Portion** Energy 279kcal/1158kJ; Protein 25.6g; Carbohydrate 1.9g, of which sugars 1.9g; Fat 18.7g, of which saturates 5.3g; Cholesterol 65mg; Calcium 8mg; Fibre 0g; Sodium 564mg.

# JAVANESE GOAT CURRY

*THROUGHOUT INDONESIA, LEAN GOAT'S MEAT IS MORE COMMONLY USED THAN LAMB OR MUTTON, ALTHOUGH LAMB COULD BE USED AS A SUBSTITUTE IN THIS RECIPE. SLOW-COOKED ON THE HOB WITH LOTS OF PUNGENT SPICES, THE TENDER, TASTY GOAT'S MEAT IS CUSTOMARILY SERVED WITH RICE AND A PICKLE OR SAMBAL. THIS RECIPE IS FROM JAVA, WHERE THE DISH IS ALSO KNOWN AS GULAI KAMBING, BUT THERE ARE MANY LOCAL VARIATIONS THROUGHOUT THE INDONESIAN ARCHIPELAGO.*

### SERVES FOUR

### INGREDIENTS
    30ml/2 tbsp palm, coconut
        or groundnut (peanut) oil
    10ml/2 tsp terasi (Indonesian
        shrimp paste)
    15ml/1 tbsp palm sugar (jaggery)
    5ml/1 tsp coriander seeds
    5ml/1 tsp cumin seeds
    2.5ml/½ tsp grated nutmeg
    2.5ml/½ tsp ground black pepper
    2–3 lemon grass stalks, halved
        and bruised
    700g/1lb 9oz boneless shoulder or
        leg of goat, or lamb, cut into
        bitesize pieces
    400g/14oz can coconut milk
    200ml/7fl oz/¾ cup water (if needed)
    12 yard-long beans
    1 bunch fresh coriander (cilantro)
        leaves, roughly chopped
    salt
For the spice paste
    2–3 shallots, chopped
    2–3 garlic cloves, chopped
    3–4 fresh chillies, seeded
        and chopped
    25g/1oz fresh galangal, chopped
    40g/1½oz fresh turmeric, chopped,
        or 10ml/2 tsp ground turmeric
    1 lemon grass stalk, chopped
    2–3 candlenuts, finely ground
To serve
    cooked rice
    2–3 fresh chillies, seeded and
        finely chopped

**COOK'S TIP**
Indonesians love strong culinary tastes and odours, but if you find the taste and smell of goat's meat a little too strong, then blanch it in boiling water for 10 minutes and drain it before adding it to the curry pot.

**1** Grind the spice paste ingredients to a coarse paste using a mortar and pestle or an electric food processor or blender.

**2** Heat 15ml/1 tbsp of the oil in a heavy pan, then stir in the spice paste and fry until it is fragrant and beginning to colour.

**3** Add the terasi and palm sugar and continue to stir-fry for 1–2 minutes, until the paste has deepened in colour but is not too dark.

**4** Heat the remaining 15ml/1 tbsp oil in a large, flameproof casserole. Stir in the coriander seeds, cumin seeds, nutmeg and black pepper, then add the spice paste and lemon grass. Stir-fry for 2–3 minutes, until the mixture is dark and fragrant.

**5** Stir the meat into the pan, making sure that it is well coated in the paste.

**6** Pour in the coconut milk, bring to the boil, then reduce the heat, cover and simmer gently for about 3 hours, until the meat is very tender. Check the meat from time to time and add the water a little at a time if the curry becomes too dry.

**7** Add the yard-long beans and cook for a further 10–15 minutes until they are just tender and have taken on the flavour of the sauce. Remove the curry from the heat.

**8** Toss some of the coriander leaves into the curry, mix well and season with salt to taste.

**9** Turn the curry out into a warmed serving dish and sprinkle the remaining coriander leaves over the top. Serve with boiled or steamed rice and a bowl of chopped chillies so that diners can add heat as desired.

**Per Portion** Energy 450kcal/1877kJ; Protein 37.9g; Carbohydrate 10.8g, of which sugars 9.1g; Fat 28.7g, of which saturates 10.3g; Cholesterol 146mg; Calcium 129mg; Fibre 2.4g; Sodium 375mg.

# VEGETABLES
# AND SALADS

The beautiful climate of Indonesia produces fine

fruits and vegetables. When blended with local spices

and flavourings, they make spectacular side dishes and

main courses. This chapter features steamed, curried

and stir-fried dishes, as well as pickles and salads

that will excite and refresh any palate.

# PINEAPPLE AND COCONUT CURRY

*THIS SWEET AND SPICY CURRY FROM THE MALUKU SPICE ISLANDS BENEFITS FROM BEING MADE THE DAY BEFORE EATING, ENABLING THE DELIGHTFULLY TROPICAL FLAVOURS TO MINGLE FOR LONGER. IN INDONESIA THE CURRY IS USUALLY EATEN AT ROOM TEMPERATURE, BUT IT IS ALSO DELICIOUS SERVED PIPING HOT, ALONG WITH A BOWL OF FLUFFY WHITE RICE.*

SERVES FOUR

INGREDIENTS

1 small, firm pineapple
15ml/1 tbsp palm or coconut oil
4–6 shallots, finely chopped
2 garlic cloves, finely chopped
1 fresh red chilli, seeded and
   finely chopped
15ml/1 tbsp palm sugar (jaggery)
400ml/14fl oz/1⅔ cups coconut milk
salt and ground black pepper
1 small bunch fresh coriander
   (cilantro) leaves, to garnish

For the spice paste
4 cloves
4 cardamom pods
1 small cinnamon stick
5ml/1 tsp coriander seeds
2.5ml/½ tsp cumin seeds
5–10ml/1–2 tsp water

**COOK'S TIPS**
• If you cannot obtain jaggery or palm sugar, use regular sugar or a mild honey to sweeten the coconut milk.
• The dish will be sweet enough for some tastes without any added sugar.

**1** First make the spice paste. Using a mortar and pestle or electric spice grinder, grind all the spices to a powder. In a bowl, mix the spice powder with the water to make a paste. Set aside.

**2** Remove the skin and any woody 'eyes' from the pineapple. Cut the flesh lengthways into quarters and remove the core. Then cut each quarter into chunky slices and put aside.

**3** Heat the oil in a wok or frying pan, stir in the shallots, garlic and chilli and stir-fry until fragrant and beginning to colour. Stir in the spice paste and fry for 1 minute. Toss in the pineapple, coating them well in the spicy mixture.

**4** Stir the sugar into the coconut milk and pour the mixture into the wok. Stir and bring to the boil. Reduce the heat and simmer for 3–4 minutes to thicken the sauce, but do not allow the pineapple to become too soft. Season to taste. Tip the curry into a warmed dish and garnish with the coriander. Serve hot or at room temperature.

**Per Portion** Energy 135kcal/573kJ; Protein 1.6g; Carbohydrate 25.4g, of which sugars 23.6g; Fat 3.8g, of which saturates 0.5g; Cholesterol 0mg; Calcium 87mg; Fibre 2.9g; Sodium 131mg.

# YOUNG JACKFRUIT CURRY

*THIS CREAMY, SWEET CURRY IS A REAL DELIGHT AND FULL OF AUTHENTIC INDONESIAN FLAVOURS.*
*IT IS PARTICULARLY GOOD TO SERVE AS PART OF A SELECTION OF CURRIES, AS ITS SWEETNESS OFFSETS*
*THE SPICY AND SAVOURY FLAVOURS OF OTHER DISHES VERY WELL. IF SERVING IT AS A VEGETARIAN*
*MAIN COURSE IT NEEDS NOTHING BUT PLAIN RICE OR BREAD AS AN ACCOMPANIMENT.*

SERVES FOUR

INGREDIENTS

  75ml/5 tbsp vegetable oil
  450g/1lb prepared young jackfruit
  400ml/14fl oz/1⅔ cups coconut milk
  5ml/1 tsp salt
  15ml/1 tbsp lime juice
  1.5ml/¼ tsp demerara (raw) sugar
  cooked rice or bread, to serve
For the spice paste
  1 large onion, chopped
  3 garlic cloves, chopped
  6 fresh red chillies, seeded
    and chopped
  2 lemon grass stalks, chopped
  2.5ml/½ tsp black peppercorns
  10g/¼ oz terasi (Indonesian
    shrimp paste)
  10g/¼oz fresh turmeric, peeled
    and chopped

**1** Grind the spice paste ingredients to a fine paste using a mortar and pestle or an electric food processor.

**2** Heat the oil in a wok or heavy frying pan and fry the spice paste over a low heat until it releases its fragrances. This should take about 4 minutes.

**VARIATIONS**
• Some variations to this dish feature bamboo shoots and tapioca leaves, which you would add at step 4.
• For a more substantial main dish you can also add a few chunks of sweet potato, but par-boil this for 5 minutes before adding it to the coconut milk.

**3** Quarter, wash and drain the prepared jackfruit, then cut it into bitesize chunks using a sharp knife. Discard any of the fibrous pith and stones (pits). Place the jackfruit pieces into a heavy pan.

**4** Add the coconut milk with the spice paste, salt, lime juice and demerara sugar to the jackfruit and stir.

**5** Bring to the boil, then simmer for 10 minutes. Serve hot with rice or bread.

**Per Portion** Energy 173kcal/719kJ; Protein 3.9g; Carbohydrate 7.3g, of which sugars 6.9g; Fat 14.5g, of which saturates 1.8g; Cholesterol 19mg; Calcium 132mg; Fibre 1.5g; Sodium 833mg.

# CABBAGE CURRY

*THIS IS A SIMPLE DISH WITH PEASANT ORIGINS. CABBAGE IS COOKED WITH COCONUT MILK AND VARYING BLENDS OF SPICES DEPENDING ON THE REGION: IN SUMATRA IT IS SUBTLE, WHILE IN BALI IT CAN BE VERY FIERY. YOU CAN USE THE BALINESE SPICE PASTE BESE GADE, OR SHALLOT AND LEMON GRASS SAMBAL, DEPENDING ON YOUR TASTE.*

SERVES FOUR

INGREDIENTS
1 whole cabbage
45ml/3 tbsp Shallot and Lemon Grass
  Sambal (see page 18)
350ml/12fl oz/scant 1½ cups
  coconut milk

5ml/1 tsp salt
2.5ml/½ tsp sugar
3 salam leaves (Indonesian
  bay leaves)

**1** Cut the cabbage into small pieces, removing the tough core, then blanch in boiling water for 2 minutes.

**2** Combine the remaining ingredients in a wok and bring to the boil. Add the cabbage and simmer for 15 minutes.

**COOK'S TIP**
For added bulk, cut a square of firm tofu into triangles and add the pieces in the last 5 minutes of cooking.

Per Portion Energy 97kcal/406kJ; Protein 3.9g; Carbohydrate 17.9g, of which sugars 17.5g; Fat 1.3g, of which saturates 0.3g; Cholesterol 1mg; Calcium 151mg; Fibre 5.3g; Sodium 629mg.

# SPICY VEGETABLES IN COCONUT MILK

*THIS DELICIOUS COMBINATION OF VEGETABLES COOKED IN COCONUT MILK AND SPICES, USUALLY ACCOMPANIES THE INDONESIAN STAPLE OF COMPRESSED RICE (LONTONG). IT SERVES WELL AS A FLAVOURSOME MAIN DISH SINCE THE SAUCE ENRICHES PLAIN RICE BEAUTIFULLY. THE CLASSIC VEGETABLES TO USE ARE AUBERGINE, CABBAGE, CAULIFLOWER AND LONG BEANS.*

SERVES FOUR

INGREDIENTS
  200g/7oz cauliflower
  1 purple aubergine (eggplant)
    or 2 brinjals
  5 yard-long or green beans
  200g/7oz cabbage
  30ml/2 tbsp vegetable oil
  450ml/16fl oz/scant 2 cups
    coconut milk
  2.5ml/½ tsp salt
  2.5ml/½ tsp sugar
For the spice paste
  4 dried chillies, soaked in warm
    water until soft
  5 shallots, chopped
  3 garlic cloves, chopped
  4 candlenuts
  5g/⅛oz fresh turmeric, peeled
  3 thin slices fresh galangal
  10g/⅓oz terasi (Indonesian shrimp paste)
  2 lemon grass stalks, 5cm/2in of
    root end chopped

**1** Slice the cauliflower, aubergine, yard-long beans and cabbage into bitesize pieces. Wash and drain.

**2** Grind the spice paste ingredients to a fine paste using a mortar and pestle or a food processor or blender. Heat the oil in a wok or frying pan and fry the paste for 4 minutes until the oil separates.

**3** Transfer the fried spices to a pan and add the coconut milk, salt and sugar. Bring to the boil and add the vegetables. Cook for 15 minutes until all the vegetables are soft.

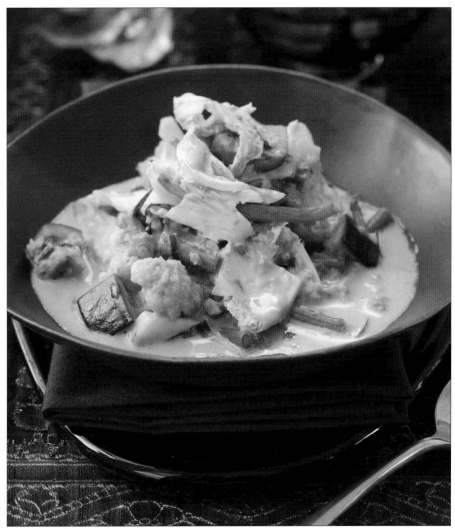

**Per Portion** Energy 59kcal/248kJ; Protein 2.2g; Carbohydrate 11.3g, of which sugars 10.9g; Fat 0.9g, of which saturates 0.3g; Cholesterol 0mg; Calcium 105mg; Fibre 4.8g; Sodium 175mg.

# PICKLED WATER SPINACH

*KANGKUNG OR WATER SPINACH IS GENERALLY STIR-FRIED BUT LENDS ITSELF TO PICKLING VERY WELL. THIS RECIPE CALLS FOR ONLY THE STALKS, WHICH REMAIN FAIRLY WHOLE, FIRM AND STILL CRUNCHY. IT IS A ROBUST SIDE DISH THAT COMPLEMENTS FRIED OR GRILLED SEAFOODS.*

**2** Split each stalk and cut into small pieces about 5cm/2in long. Wash and drain, and dry handfuls on kitchen paper.

**3** Sprinkle the stalks with salt and leave for 20 minutes. Squeeze out the moisture with your hands.

**4** Combine the pickling solution ingredients in a large, heavy pan or earthenware pot and simmer until the sugar is completely dissolved. Remove from the heat to cool completely.

SERVES FOUR

INGREDIENTS
  675g/1½lb water spinach (kangkung)
  10ml/2 tsp salt
For the pickling solution
  4 garlic cloves, crushed
  50g/2oz sugar
  200ml/7fl oz/¾ cup coconut
    vinegar
  5ml/1 tsp salt

**COOK'S TIP**
Use the pickled water spinach within
3 days of making it.

**1** Wash and drain the water spinach stalks after trimming away the leaves. The yield will be about 600g/1¼lb.

**5** Pour the solution over the kangkung, toss well to coat, and store in a preserving jar for a day or two before serving with grilled (broiled) poultry or seafood.

**Per Portion** Energy 96kcal/405kJ; Protein 5.2g; Carbohydrate 16.6g, of which sugars 15.7g; Fat 1.4g, of which saturates 0.2g; Cholesterol 0mg; Calcium 295mg; Fibre 3.8g; Sodium 729mg.

# WATER SPINACH IN TANGY SAUCE

*THERE ARE FEW ASIAN VEGETABLES THAT CAN MATCH WATER SPINACH (KANGKUNG) FOR FLAVOUR, TEXTURE AND VERSATILITY. AFTER A SUMMER SHOWER, IT GROWS IN SWAMPY LAND LIKE A WEED. THIS DISH, THEREFORE, IS HIGHLY ECONOMICAL FOR INDONESIAN COOKS — AND VERY DELICIOUS.*

SERVES FOUR

INGREDIENTS
   600g/1lb 6oz water
     spinach (kangkung)
   30ml/2 tbsp oil
   4 garlic cloves, crushed
   200g/7oz minced (ground) pork
   200g/7oz small fresh prawns
     (shrimp), peeled
   200ml/7fl oz/¾ cup water
   100ml/3½fl oz/⅓ cup coconut
     vinegar
   5ml/1 tsp salt

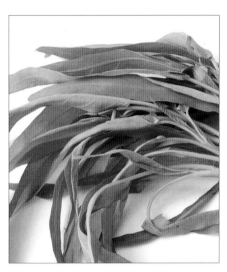

**3** Add the prawns, spinach stems, water, coconut vinegar and salt. Braise over a high heat, stirring to incorporate all the ingredients, for 3–4 minutes, then fold in the water spinach leaves. Serve hot.

**1** Wash the water spinach well. Pinch off the leaves and slice the stalks thinly.

**2** Heat the oil and fry the garlic until light brown, then add the pork. Fry for 4 minutes until cooked through.

**COOK'S TIPS**
• Water spinach grows in brackish or swampy water, so slice the hollow stems through to see if there is any mud inside.
• Water spinach contains a lot of water, so if you prefer a dry dish, reduce the amount of water by half.

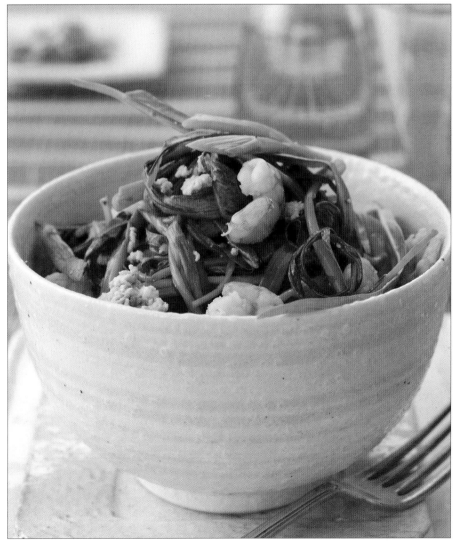

**Per Portion** Energy 207kcal/861kJ; Protein 22.6g; Carbohydrate 2.4g, of which sugars 2.3g; Fat 11.9g, of which saturates 2.7g; Cholesterol 131mg; Calcium 298mg; Fibre 3.2g; Sodium 829mg.

# STEAMED VEGETABLES AND FRUIT WITH PEANUT SAUCE

*THIS CLASSIC INDONESIAN DISH OF VEGETABLES IN A PEANUT SAUCE, KNOWN AS GADO GADO, IS ENJOYED THROUGHOUT THE ISLANDS, WHICH MEANS THERE ARE MANY VARIATIONS AS EACH REGION WILL INCORPORATE THEIR LOCAL VEGETABLES AND FRUIT. SERVED AT ROOM TEMPERATURE WITH A BOWL OF RICE, THIS DISH COULD BE AN APPETIZER OR A MEAL ON ITS OWN.*

### SERVES FOUR TO SIX

INGREDIENTS
  corn oil, for deep-frying
  500g/1¼lb tofu block, cut
    into 4 rectangular pieces
  4 shallots, finely sliced
  3 carrots, sliced diagonally
  12 yard-long beans, cut into
    bitesize pieces
  225g/8oz water spinach (kangkung),
    washed and thinly sliced
  1 firm mango, pitted and cut into
    bitesize chunks
  ½ pineapple, cored and cut into
    bitesize chunks
  225g/8oz mung beansprouts
  2 hard-boiled eggs, quartered
  salt
For the peanut sauce
  30ml/2 tbsp coconut or
    groundnut (peanut) oil
  3 shallots, finely chopped
  3 garlic cloves, finely chopped
  3–4 fresh red chillies, seeded and
    finely chopped
  175g/6oz/1 cup unsalted roasted
    peanuts, finely ground
  15g/½oz fresh galangal or
    root ginger, finely chopped
  5–10ml/1–2 tsp terasi
    (Indonesian shrimp paste)
  15ml/1 tbsp palm sugar
    (jaggery)
  600ml/1 pint/2½ cups
    coconut milk
  juice of 1 lime
  30ml/2 tbsp kecap manis
    (Indonesian sweet soy sauce)

**COOK'S TIPS**
• Other ingredients commonly used for gado gado include shredded cabbage, sweet potato, turnip, papaya and star fruit (carambola).
• If you cannot obtain yard-long beans, French or green beans can be used instead.

**1** First make the peanut sauce. Heat the oil in a wok or heavy pan, stir in the shallots, garlic and chillies and fry until fragrant and beginning to colour.

**2** Add the peanuts, galangal, terasi and palm sugar and fry for about 4 minutes, until the peanuts begin to darken and ooze a little oil.

**3** Pour the coconut milk, lime juice and kecap manis into the pan and bring to the boil. Reduce the heat and simmer gently for 15–20 minutes, until the sauce has reduced a little and thickened. Leave to cool.

**4** Heat enough oil in a wok or large pan for deep-frying, add the rectangular tofu pieces one at a time and fry the tofu until it is a light golden brown colour.

**5** Using a slotted spoon, remove the tofu from the pan and drain on kitchen paper. Cut the tofu into slices and set aside.

**6** Heat 15ml/1 tbsp of the oil from the deep-frying in a small, heavy pan, add the shallots and fry until deep golden in colour. Drain on crumpled kitchen paper and put aside.

**7** Fill a large pan a third of the way up with water and place a steamer basket over it. Bring the water to the boil and put the carrots and yard-long beans in the basket. Put the lid on, reduce the heat and steam for 3–4 minutes.

**8** Add the water spinach to the steamer for a minute, then drain the vegetables and refresh under cold running water.

**9** Put the vegetables in a bowl. Add the mango, pineapple and beansprouts and pour in half the peanut sauce. Toss well and transfer to a serving dish. Arrange the egg quarters and tofu slices and drizzle the remaining peanut sauce over the top. Sprinkle with the reserved fried shallots to garnish.

**Per Portion** Energy 449kcal/1873kJ; Protein 22.2g; Carbohydrate 24.5g, of which sugars 20.7g; Fat 30g, of which saturates 5.1g; Cholesterol 108mg; Calcium 611mg; Fibre 5.1g; Sodium 675mg.

# SPICED STEAMED CAULIFLOWER

*THIS INDONESIAN RECIPE IS A GREAT WAY TO SERVE CAULIFLOWER, GIVING IT SOME MUCH-NEEDED PUNCHY FLAVOUR AND A WARM COLOUR. THE BEAUTIFUL CRUNCHINESS OF THE VEGETABLE IS RETAINED, AS ARE THE NUTRIENTS, BY COOKING IT IN A STEAMER.*

**2** Place the cauliflower florets in to a large mixing bowl with the ground cloves and cinnamon, and toss together well.

**3** Add the garlic purée, sesame oil and salt, and stir until evenly mixed.

**4** Transfer the cauliflower to a bamboo steamer and steam for 20 minutes, until the cauliflower is tender.

**5** Once cooked, the cauliflower can be served warm or cold and makes a perfect accompaniment to any curry.

SERVES FOUR

INGREDIENTS
   600g/1lb 6oz cauliflower
   pinch of ground cloves
   pinch of ground cinnamon
   30g/2 tbsp garlic purée (paste)
   30ml/2 tbsp sesame oil
   2.5ml/½ tsp salt

**1** Break the cauliflower into small florets, then wash and drain the pieces.

**Per Portion** Energy 108kcal/447kJ; Protein 6g; Carbohydrate 5.7g, of which sugars 3.9g; Fat 6.9g, of which saturates 1.1g; Cholesterol 0mg; Calcium 34mg; Fibre 3g; Sodium 260mg.

# AUBERGINES IN A CHILLI SAUCE

*THIS DISH IS A GREAT INDONESIAN FAVOURITE, BOTH IN THE HOME AND AT THE STREET STALL. YOU CAN MAKE IT WITH LARGE AUBERGINES, CUT IN HALF AND BAKED, OR WITH SMALL ONES, BUTTERFLIED. THE SPICY FILLING AND MELTINGLY SOFT AUBERGINE FLESH ARE EXCELLENT WITH RICE OR BREAD.*

SERVES FOUR

INGREDIENTS
    2 large aubergines (eggplants), cut in
      half lengthways, or 4 small
      aubergines, butterflied
    45ml/3 tbsp coconut oil
    400g/14oz can tomatoes, drained
    5ml/1 tsp palm sugar (jaggery)
    juice of 2 limes
    salt
    1 small bunch fresh coriander
      (cilantro), to garnish
For the spice paste
    4 shallots, finely chopped
    4 garlic cloves, finely chopped
    25g/1oz fresh root ginger,
      finely chopped
    3–4 fresh red chillies, seeded and
      finely chopped

**1** Preheat the oven to 180°C/350°F/ Gas 4. Put the prepared aubergines on a baking tray and brush with 30ml/2 tbsp of the coconut oil. Bake in the oven for 40 minutes, until soft and tender.

**2** Grind the spice paste ingredients to a coarse paste using a mortar and pestle or an electric food processor or blender.

**3** Heat the remaining oil in a wok, stir in the spice paste and cook for 1–2 minutes.

**4** Add the tomatoes and sugar and cook for 3–4 minutes, then stir in the lime juice and a little salt to taste.

**5** Put the baked aubergines on a serving dish and press down the flesh to form a dip, using the back of a wooden spoon.

**6** Spoon the tomato sauce into the dip and then spoon it over the aubergines.

**7** Garnish with the coriander leaves and serve the aubergines hot or at room temperature.

**Per Portion** Energy 100kcal/419kJ; Protein 2.1g; Carbohydrate 9.4g, of which sugars 8.8g; Fat 6.4g, of which saturates 0.9g; Cholesterol 0mg; Calcium 42mg; Fibre 3.7g; Sodium 15mg.

# PEPPERED YARD-LONG BEANS

*THROUGHOUT INDONESIA, VEGETABLES ARE AN ESSENTIAL PART OF EVERY MEAL. INDONESIAN COOKS ARE ADEPT AT ENHANCING THE FAIRLY NEUTRAL FLAVOUR OF BASIC VEGETABLES BY COOKING THEM WITH DIFFERENT BLENDS OF SPICES AND AROMATICS. THIS IS A GREAT WAY TO PREPARE SIMPLE GREEN BEANS; THE FRESH, SPICY FLAVOURS TRANSFORMS THEM INTO A REAL TREAT.*

SERVES FOUR

INGREDIENTS
   400g/14oz yard-long beans
   15ml/1 tbsp vegetable oil
   4 shallots
   1.5ml/¼ tsp ground turmeric
   1.5ml/¼ tsp ground black pepper
   1 lemon grass stalk, 5cm/2in of root
     end finely sliced
   5ml/1 tsp palm sugar (jaggery)
   2 fresh red chillies
   5ml/1 tsp salt
   10g/⅓oz terasi (Indonesian
     shrimp paste)
   75ml/5 tbsp coconut milk

**1** Wash, top and tail the beans and cut each into 2–3 pieces. Peel and finely chop the shallots. Slice the chillies finely (do not seed them unless you want a mild dish).

**2** Heat the oil and fry the shallots for 2 minutes. Add the turmeric, black pepper, lemon grass, sugar, chillies and salt and stir for 2 minutes.

**3** Add the prepared beans and stir for a further minute.

**4** Add the terasi and coconut milk and simmer for 8 minutes, stirring well. Serve warm, as coconut milk congeals when it gets cold.

**COOK'S TIP**
This dish keeps well, so you can prepare it ahead and warm it through for serving the next day.

**Per Portion** Energy 68kcal/284kJ; Protein 3.5g; Carbohydrate 6.4g, of which sugars 5.1g; Fat 3.4g, of which saturates 0.5g; Cholesterol 13mg; Calcium 76mg; Fibre 2.4g; Sodium 130mg.

# YARD-LONG BEANS IN COCONUT SAUCE

*HIGHLY VERSATILE YARD-LONG BEANS ARE ALSO KNOWN AS SNAKE BEANS. FRENCH, GREEN OR DWARF BEANS CAN BE USED IF YOU CANNOT FIND YARD-LONG BEANS. THEY CAN BE EATEN RAW BUT ARE BEST LIGHTLY COOKED. KNOWN AS BUAH CACANG IN INDONESIA, THEY ARE USED IN MANY WAYS: FRIED, BOILED AND IN CURRIES. THIS LIGHT SOUPY RECIPE MAKES AN EXCELLENT SIDE DISH.*

SERVES FOUR

INGREDIENTS

    400g/14oz yard-long or green beans
    2 lemon grass stalks
    350ml/12fl oz/scant 1½ cups
      coconut milk
    30g/2 tbsp Balinese Spice Paste
      (see page 18)
    5ml/1 tsp salt
    3 salam leaves (Indonesian
      bay leaves)
    1.5ml/¼ tsp sugar
    fried shallots, to garnish
    cooked rice, to serve

**3** Combine the coconut milk with the spice paste, salt, salam leaves, lemon grass and sugar in a heavy pan.

**4** Add the beans and cook over a high heat until the sauce is creamy. Garnish with fried shallots and serve with rice.

**1** Cut the yard-long beans into 5cm/2in lengths, then wash and drain.

**2** Bruise the lemon grass stalks by hitting them with a meat tenderizer.

**COOK'S TIP**
You can make a more complex vegetable dish by combining 120g/5oz each of yard-long beans, spinach and cabbage instead of just beans. Add the spinach in the last two minutes of cooking.

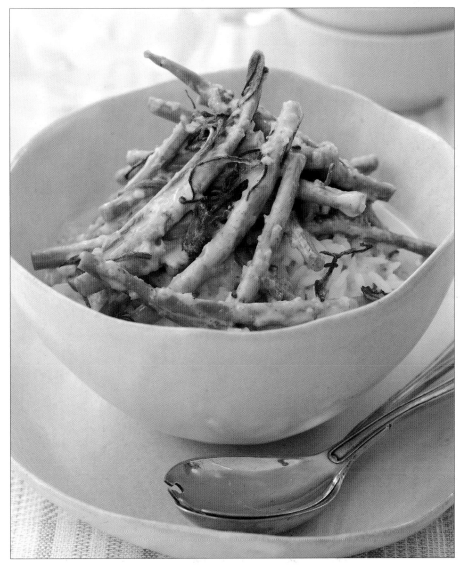

Per Portion Energy 50kcal/208kJ; Protein 2.5g; Carbohydrate 7.4g, of which sugars 6.4g; Fat 1.5g, of which saturates 0.3g; Cholesterol 1mg; Calcium 65mg; Fibre 2.3g; Sodium 594mg.

# STIR-FRIED MIXED VEGETABLES

*CAP CAI CA IS A SINO-INDONESIAN STIR-FRY; THE NAME IS A PHONETIC SPELLING FROM THE FUJIAN DIALECT, WHICH LITERALLY MEANS 'TEN VEGETABLES FRY' BUT ACTUALLY ALLUDES TO ANY MULTIPLE-VEGETABLE DISH. THIS CHINESE RECIPE HAS BEEN ABSORBED INTO THE INDONESIAN CULINARY LEXICON AND IS FEATURED ON MANY LOCAL RESTAURANT MENUS.*

SERVES FOUR

INGREDIENTS
    200g/7oz pak choi (bok choy)
    16 mangetouts (snow peas)
    200g/7oz canned bamboo
        shoot slices
    30ml/2 tbsp vegetable oil
    3 garlic cloves, crushed
    16 water chestnuts
    8 Chinese mushrooms, soaked
        until soft, sliced
    15ml/1 tbsp light soy sauce
    15ml/1 tbsp oyster sauce
    15ml/1 tbsp sesame oil
    2.5ml/½ tsp ground black pepper
    105ml/7 tbsp water
    10ml/2 tsp cornflour (cornstarch)

**1** Cut the pak choi leaves into short lengths. Trim the tops and tails of the mangetouts.

**2** Wash and drain the bamboo shoots to remove some of the canning liquid scent, which can be overpowering.

**3** Heat the oil and fry the garlic over a low heat until golden brown, then add the pak choi, mangetouts, bamboo shoots, water chestnuts and mushrooms. Stir-fry over a high heat for 3 minutes.

**4** Add the soy sauce, oyster sauce, sesame oil and black pepper to the pan and continue to stir well, coating all the vegetables in each flavouring.

**5** Mix the water with the cornflour to form a smooth, thin blend and pour into the pan. Stir over a medium-high heat until the sauce is fairly thick, then serve the dish immediately with noodles or rice or as a vegetable side dish.

**Per Portion** Energy 84kcal/352kJ; Protein 5.4g; Carbohydrate 7.9g, of which sugars 4.2g; Fat 3.6g, of which saturates 0.5g; Cholesterol 0mg; Calcium 121mg; Fibre 3.2g; Sodium 610mg.

# MIXED SALAD <u>WITH</u> COCONUT

*URABS ARE TRADITIONAL INDONESIAN SALAD OR VEGETABLE DISHES, WHICH MAY USE A RANGE OF COOKED OR RAW INGREDIENTS. MANY CALL FOR DIFFERENT VEGETABLES BUT YOU CAN ALSO USE JUST ONE IF TIME DOES NOT PERMIT THE PREPARATION OF A MORE COMPLEX DISH. THE DRESSING IS GOOD WITH MANY VEGETABLE DISHES, SO CONSIDER MAKING A BATCH FOR USE ANOTHER DAY.*

SERVES FOUR

INGREDIENTS
- 115g/4oz cabbage
- 100g/3½oz spinach
- 100g/3½oz beansprouts
- 15ml/1 tbsp desiccated (dry unsweetened shredded) coconut
- 30g/2 tbsp shallots, to garnish
- 2 fresh red chillies, seeded and sliced

For the dressing
- 30ml/2 tbsp garlic purée (paste)
- 1 fresh red chilli, finely chopped
- juice of 3 limes
- 1 lemon grass stalk, 5cm/2in of root end, finely sliced
- 4cm/1.5in piece lesser galangal, finely chopped
- 1.5ml/¼ tsp salt
- 2.5ml/½ tsp ground black pepper
- 2.5ml/½ tsp sugar
- 15ml/1 tbsp olive oil

**1** Cut the cabbage into thin strips and blanch in a pan of boiling water for 2 minutes. Drain.

**2** Blanch the spinach as in step 1. Wash and drain the beansprouts.

**3** Dry-fry the desiccated coconut for 3 minutes over a low–medium heat until golden brown. Set aside.

**VARIATION**
Introduce a fruity flavour by reducing the amount of each vegetable slightly and adding some sliced green mango strips at step 4.

**4** Fry the shallots for the garnish until crisp and golden. Drain off any excess oil on kitchen paper and set aside.

**5** Use your hands to gently mix the cabbage, spinach, beansprouts and chillies in a salad bowl.

**6** Add the dressing ingredients to a jar and shake well to blend. Pour the dressing over the vegetables and toss for an even coating. Garnish the salad with fried shallots and the dry-fried coconut before serving.

**Per Portion** Energy 141kcal/585kJ; Protein 4.5g; Carbohydrate 6.4g, of which sugars 5.1g; Fat 11g, of which saturates 9.1g; Cholesterol 8mg; Calcium 54mg; Fibre 4.6g; Sodium 86mg.

# RAW VEGETABLE AND COCONUT SALAD

*THIS INDONESIAN SALAD IS A TYPICAL DISH THAT IS SERVED AS A SNACK WITH RICE ON A BANANA LEAF OR WITH FISH AND MEAT. STREET STALLS OFTEN PREPARE A SIMPLE SALAD OF THIS KIND TO ACCOMPANY THE MAIN DISH. THE INGREDIENTS OF THE SALAD VARY WITH THE SEASONS.*

### SERVES FOUR TO SIX

INGREDIENTS
- 225g/8oz yard-long or green beans, cut into bitesize pieces
- 3–4 tomatoes, skinned, seeded and cut into bitesize chunks
- 4–6 spring onions (scallions), sliced
- 225g/8oz beansprouts
- ½ fresh coconut, grated

For the dressing
- 1–2 fresh red or green chillies, seeded and chopped
- 2 garlic cloves, chopped
- 25g/1oz galangal or fresh root ginger, grated
- 5–10ml/1–2 tsp terasi (Indonesian shrimp paste)
- juice of 2–3 limes
- salt and ground black pepper

**1** To make the dressing, using a mortar and pestle, grind the chillies, garlic and galangal or ginger to a paste. Add the terasi and juice of 2 limes. If the limes are not juicy, then squeeze the juice of the extra lime and add to the dressing, or add a little water, so that it is of pouring consistency. Season the dressing with salt and pepper to taste.

**2** Put the yard-long beans, tomatoes, spring onions, beansprouts and grated coconut into a large bowl. Using your fingers or two spoons, mix the ingredients together thoroughly.

**3** Toss the dressing into the salad with clean hands, transfer to a bowl and serve immediately.

**Per Portion** Energy 141kcal/584kJ; Protein 4.5g; Carbohydrate 6.4g, of which sugars 5.1g; Fat 11g, of which saturates 9.1g; Cholesterol 8mg; Calcium 54mg; Fibre 4.6g; Sodium 86mg.

# GREEN PAPAYA SALAD

*THROUGHOUT SOUTH-EAST ASIA, GREEN PAPAYAS HAVE EARNED HUGE POPULARITY FOR THE UNIQUE TEXTURE AND FLAVOUR THEY LEND TO SALADS. THIS IS NOT A SALAD TO BE REGARDED AS A MERE SIDESHOW, BUT AS A FEATURE DISH THAT IS SATISFYING YET LIGHT.*

SERVES FOUR

INGREDIENTS
2 green papayas, seeded
  and grated
4 shallots, finely sliced
1–2 fresh red chillies, seeded, halved
  lengthways and finely sliced
150g/5oz/1 cup plump sultanas
  (golden raisins) or raisins
2 garlic cloves, crushed
25g/1oz fresh root ginger, grated
45–60ml/3–4 tbsp coconut vinegar
  or cane vinegar
50g/2oz palm sugar (jaggery)
coriander (cilantro) leaves, to garnish

**1** Put the papaya, shallots, chillies, sultanas, garlic and ginger into a bowl. In a separate small bowl, mix together the coconut vinegar and palm sugar until the sugar has dissolved.

**2** Pour the sweet vinegar mixture over the salad and toss well together. Leave the salad to marinate for at least 1 hour or, for the best flavour, in the refrigerator overnight to allow the flavours to mingle. Serve, garnished with coriander leaves.

**Per Portion** Energy 232kcal/988kJ; Protein 2.5g; Carbohydrate 58.3g, of which sugars 57.6g; Fat 0.4g, of which saturates 0g; Cholesterol 0mg; Calcium 81mg; Fibre 5.5g; Sodium 19mg.

# FRUIT SALAD IN A TANGY DRESSING

*ENTRENCHED IN THE INDONESIAN CULINARY CULTURE, RUJAK
APPEARS IN MANY GUISES — AS A SNACK, AS A SALAD TO
ACCOMPANY FRIED AND GRILLED DISHES, OR AS A FESTIVE DISH.
IN JAVA, IT IS TRADITIONALLY SERVED BEFORE THE BIRTH OF
THE FIRST CHILD. IN THE 19TH CENTURY, JAVANESE SETTLERS
INTRODUCED IT TO MALAYSIA, WHERE IT HAS BEEN ADAPTED
BY THE CHINESE, INDIANS AND MALAYS TO SUIT THEIR TASTES.
DESIGNED TO BE FLEXIBLE, THIS REFRESHING SALAD, TOSSED IN
A PUNGENT DRESSING, CAN INCLUDE ANY CHOICE OF FRUIT AND
VEGETABLES THAT YOU LIKE.*

### SERVES FOUR TO SIX

INGREDIENTS
   1 green mango, finely sliced
   1 ripe, firm papaya, finely sliced
   1–2 star fruit (carambola),
     finely sliced
   ½ pineapple, finely sliced and cut
     into bitesize pieces
   ½ pomelo, segmented
   1 small cucumber, roughly peeled,
     seeded and finely sliced
   1 yam bean or jicama, finely sliced
   a handful of beansprouts
For the sauce
   10ml/2 tsp terasi (Indonesian
     shrimp paste)
   225g/8oz/1½ cups roasted peanuts
   4 garlic cloves, chopped
   2–4 fresh red chillies, seeded
     and chopped
   15ml/1 tbsp tamarind paste
   30ml/2 tbsp palm sugar (jaggery)
   salt

**1** To make the sauce, dry-fry the terasi
in a small, heavy frying pan until it is
golden and emits a toasted aroma.

**2** Using a mortar and pestle or an
electric blender, pound the peanuts,
garlic and chillies to a coarse paste.
Beat in the dry-fried terasi, tamarind
paste and sugar. Add enough water to
make a thick pouring sauce, then stir
until the sugar has dissolved. Season
the sauce with salt to taste.

**3** Put all the fruit and vegetables,
except the beansprouts, into a large
bowl. Pour in some of the sauce and
toss gently together. Leave the salad to
stand for 30 minutes.

**4** Turn the salad into a serving dish.
Sprinkle the beansprouts over the top
and serve with the remaining sauce
drizzled on top.

**Per Portion** Energy 321kcal/1344kJ; Protein 12.3g; Carbohydrate 30g, of which sugars 27.2g; Fat 17.7g, of which saturates
3.3g; Cholesterol 8mg; Calcium 91mg; Fibre 6.2g; Sodium 81mg.

# SWEET SNACKS, BAKES AND DRINKS

*Indonesia offers a superb selection of special-occasion*

*sweet snacks, cakes and cookies, such as a meringue-*

*topped coconut pudding, and crumbly Rice Flour and*

*Coconut Milk Cookies. During the day, a variety of*

*cooling teas and syrupy drinks can be enjoyed, such*

*as Avocado Juice, or Fresh Ginger Tea.*

# STICKY COCONUT CREPES

*A GREAT FAVOURITE AT STREET STALLS, THIS IS ONE OF THE INDONESIAN SWEET SNACKS THAT TOURISTS IN BALI AND JAVA RAVE ABOUT. INDONESIANS LOVE THEM TOO, CONSUMING THEM IN GREAT QUANTITIES, AS THEY ARE SO SIMPLE AND TASTY. MADE WITH THE SAME BATTER THAT IS USED FOR SAVOURY SPRING ROLLS, THE CRÊPES ARE FILLED WITH A STICKY COCONUT MIXTURE AND SERVED EITHER AT ROOM TEMPERATURE OR HOT.*

SERVES THREE TO FOUR

INGREDIENTS
15ml/1 tbsp palm or coconut oil
30ml/2 tbsp corn oil
5ml/1 tsp cardamom seeds
225g/8oz/1½ cups fresh coconut,
  finely grated or shredded
60ml/4 tbsp palm sugar (jaggery)
pinch of salt
sugar, to sprinkle (optional)
For the crepes
115g/4oz/⅔ cup rice flour
30ml/2 tbsp tapioca flour or
  cornflour (cornstarch)
2 eggs, beaten
about 400ml/14fl oz/1⅔ cups water
corn or vegetable oil, for frying
salt

**1** To make the crêpes, sift the rice and tapioca flours into a bowl and make a well in the centre. Add the beaten eggs and palm oil into the well and gradually pour in the water, whisking all the time, until it forms a smooth batter. Season with salt and leave to rest for 30 minutes.

**2** Heat a heavy, non-stick pancake or crêpe pan and, using a piece of kitchen paper, wipe a little of the corn oil all over the surface. Using a small cup or ladle, add a little batter to the pan, tilting it at the same time to spread the batter evenly over the base.

**3** Reduce the heat and cook the crêpe gently until the batter sets and lifts at the edges, then flip the crêpe over and cook on the other side until just lightly browned.

**4** Carefully lift the crêpe on to a plate and repeat with the remaining batter. In total there should be enough batter to make 12 crêpes.

**5** In a heavy, non-stick pan, heat the palm or coconut oil and stir in the cardamom seeds. Toss in the coconut, and then add the sugar and salt.

**6** Over a low heat, toss the coconut continuously for 3–5 minutes, until it caramelizes. Remove from the heat and leave to cool.

**7** Place a crêpe on a flat surface in front of you and heap 15–30ml/1–2 tbsp of caramelized coconut just off centre. Fold the edge nearest to you over the filling, tuck in the sides, and roll over to form a log.

**8** Repeat with the remaining crêpes and filling.

**9** Serve the crêpes at room temperature, or heat in a lightly oiled, heavy frying pan with an extra sprinkling of sugar to make them sticky, and serve hot.

**Per Portion** Energy 475kcal/1972kJ; Protein 7g; Carbohydrate 38.6g, of which sugars 1.6g; Fat 32.4g, of which saturates 17.8g; Cholesterol 95mg; Calcium 30mg; Fibre 4.2g; Sodium 48mg.

# PANDANUS CUSTARD <u>WITH</u> GLUTINOUS RICE

*THE RICH EGG AND COCONUT MILK CUSTARD USED HERE IS TRADITIONALLY MADE AS A TOPPING FOR STEAMED GLUTINOUS RICE AND IS CALLED SRI MUKA IN INDONESIA. AS A BREAKFAST SPREAD FOR TOAST IT IS KNOWN AS KAYA. THE PANDANUS LEAVES GIVE THE GLUTINOUS RICE BASE A DELICIOUSLY SUBTLE SCENT, AND COLOUR THE CUSTARD A DELICATE GREEN.*

SERVES SIX TO EIGHT

INGREDIENTS
  200g/7oz/scant 1 cup glutinous rice,
    soaked overnight in water to cover
  200ml/7fl oz/¾ cup coconut milk
  2.5ml/½ tsp salt
  2 pandanus (screwpine) leaves
For the topping
  2 pandanus (screwpine) leaves
  6 eggs
  115g/4oz/½ cup sugar
  300ml/½ pint/1¼ cups thick
    coconut milk
  15ml/1 tbsp rice flour
  5ml/1 tsp cornflour (cornstarch)

**1** Place the soaked glutinous rice, which should have absorbed all of the water, in a steamer.

**2** Sprinkle over the coconut milk and salt. Cut up the pandanus leaves into pieces and press them all over the rice.

**3** Steam the rice until it is set but not cooked through. Remove the pandanus leaves and discard.

**4** For the topping, cut the pandanus leaves into small pieces and grind using a mortar and pestle.

**5** Squeeze out the green juice through a fine sieve (strainer) into a small bowl.

**6** Beat the eggs with the sugar for 2–3 minutes, or until the sugar is completely dissolved. Strain the mixture into a bowl.

**7** Whisk together the coconut milk, rice flour and cornflour, then pour on to the egg and sugar mixture and whisk thoroughly to make a smooth, thin custard.

**8** Stir in the pandanus juice. The mixture will have a delicate green tint.

**9** Pour the mixture into a non-stick pan and cook over a low heat for about 5 minutes until it becomes thick, beating hard with a wooden spoon to prevent lumps forming,

**10** Press the rice down to compact it. Pour the custard topping mixture on to the rice, cover and steam for 20 minutes or until the custard is set firm.

**11** Allow the dessert to cool fully before cutting it into diamond shapes to chill and serve as a snack.

**Per Portion** Energy 172kcal/721kJ; Protein 6.9g; Carbohydrate 26.2g, of which sugars 3.1g; Fat 4.5g, of which saturates 1.3g; Cholesterol 143mg; Calcium 45mg; Fibre 0g; Sodium 122mg.

# INDONESIAN BLACK STICKY RICE PUDDING

*OFTEN CALLED FORBIDDEN RICE, BLACK STICKY RICE IS USUALLY FLAVOURED WITH PANDANUS LEAVES BUT YOU CAN USE A VANILLA POD OR GINGER INSTEAD.*

SERVES FOUR TO SIX

INGREDIENTS
   225g/8oz/1 cup plus 2 tbsp
      black glutinous rice
   300ml/½ pint/1¼ cups water
   60ml/4 tbsp palm sugar (jaggery)
   2–3 pandanus (screwpine) leaves,
      1 vanilla pod (bean) or 25g/1oz
      fresh root ginger
   400g/14oz can coconut milk
   a pinch of salt
   60ml/4 tbsp desiccated (dry
      unsweetened shredded) coconut

**1** Put the rice in a large bowl, cover generously with cold water and leave to soak for 4 hours. Rinse the rice under cold running water and drain.

**2** Put the rice in a pan, cover with the measured water and bring it to the boil. Stir in 45ml/3 tbsp of the sugar until dissolved, and then add the pandanus leaves, vanilla pod or ginger. Reduce the heat and simmer for 10–15 minutes, until the water has been absorbed. Remove from the heat, cover and leave to steam for 10 minutes.

**3** Meanwhile, pour the coconut milk into a separate pan and bring to the boil. Stir in the remaining sugar mixture and the salt until the sugar has dissolved.

**4** In a small, heavy frying pan, quickly dry-fry the coconut, tossing it all the time, until it gives off a lovely aroma and turns golden brown. Turn it into a bowl.

**5** Remove the pandanus leaves, vanilla pod or ginger from the rice and spoon the pudding into individual bowls. Drizzle the hot coconut milk over the top and sprinkle with the coconut.

**Per Portion** Energy 249kcal/1044kJ; Protein 4g; Carbohydrate 42.5g, of which sugars 14.4g; Fat 7g, of which saturates 5.5g; Cholesterol 0mg; Calcium 33mg; Fibre 1.4g; Sodium 78mg.

# YOUNG COCONUT PUDDING

*PODENG (FROM THE DISH'S NAME OF PODENG KELAPA MUDA) IS THE INDONESIAN TRANSLITERATION OF THE 'PUDDING', AND THIS ONE IS ALMOST WESTERN IN CONCEPT BUT FOR THE COCONUT.*

SERVES FOUR

INGREDIENTS
   6 egg yolks
   115g/4oz sugar
   ¼ tsp vanilla extract
   65g/2½oz/9 tbsp plain
     (all-purpose) flour
   90ml/6 tbsp sweetened
     condensed milk
   120ml/4fl oz/½ cup warm water
   250g/9oz young coconut meat,
     finely chopped
For the meringue
   6 egg whites
   15ml/1 tbsp caster (superfine) sugar
   pinch of salt
   65g/2½ oz flaked (sliced) and
     toasted almonds

**1** Preheat the oven to 200°C/400°F/Gas 6. Put the yolks, sugar and vanilla extract in a large bowl and whisk until slightly frothy.

**2** Gradually add the plain flour to the condensed milk and water in a medium pan, mixing constantly to blend well.

**3** Add the coconut meat into the flour and milk mixture and combine well. Then stir in the prepared egg yolk and sugar mixture.

**4** Cook over a low heat, stirring with a wooden spoon, until the mixture thickens, about 5 minutes. Pour the mixture into a greased ovenproof dish.

**5** Put the egg whites in a clean, grease-free bowl and whisk until white and stiffening, using an electric whisk if you prefer.

**6** Add the sugar and salt and continue to whisk until stiff peaks form.

**7** Spread the meringue over the coconut mixture, and bake for 15–20 minutes, until the topping turns pale golden. Top with the flaked and toasted almonds and serve at room temperature.

**Per Portion** Energy 668kcal/2791kJ; Protein 17.2g; Carbohydrate 58.4g, of which sugars 45.6g; Fat 42.3g, of which saturates 24.1g; Cholesterol 308mg; Calcium 169mg; Fibre 6.9g; Sodium 141mg.

# RICE FLOUR AND COCONUT MILK COOKIES

*THESE INDONESIAN FESTIVE TREATS ARE ALSO POPULAR THROUGHOUT SOUTH-EAST ASIA. THE LITTLE CRUMBLY BITES ARE MADE FROM A BLEND OF RICE AND TAPIOCA FLOUR, AND MAY BE CUT INTO PRETTY SHAPES WITH SPECIAL CUTTERS. A FINE TOUCH IS TO SPRINKLE THEM WITH SESAME SEEDS.*

SERVES SIX TO EIGHT

INGREDIENTS
    400g/14oz/2 cups tapioca flour
    200g/7oz/generous 1 cup
      rice flour
    200g/7oz/1 cup sugar
    250ml/8fl oz/1 cup thick
      coconut milk
    3 egg yolks
    1 egg white
    1 tsp baking powder
    1 egg, beaten
    sesame seeds (optional)

**1** Mix both flours and dry in a wok over a very low heat. This is an important step to remove any moisture that is still in the flour. In Indonesia, it is simply dried in the sun for a few hours.

**2** Mix the sugar and coconut milk and simmer for 5 minutes on low heat. Remove from the heat and allow to cool.

**3** Beat the egg yolks and egg white separately until frothy, and add to the coconut milk mixture. Whisk for a few minutes but do not over-beat, as the cookies should not be full of air.

**4** Sift the dry flour and baking powder into a large bowl. Make a well in the centre and pour in the egg and coconut milk mixture. Stir well, then knead into a soft dough. If the dough is too wet, add a little more tapioca flour. It should be dryish but not falling apart, and come away from the bowl easily.

**5** Roll out the dough on a floured board to about 1cm/½in thick. Use cutters to make different shapes or make little rounded cookies by hand, each about 2.5 cm/1in in diameter.

**6** Dust a baking sheet with a little tapioca flour. Place the cookies on the sheet, brush with a little beaten egg and sprinkle with sesame seeds, if desired.

**7** Preheat the oven to 180°C/350°F/ Gas 4 and bake each batch for about 12–15 minutes until pale golden but not brown.

**8** Transfer to a cooling rack and leave to cool. Store in an airtight jar. They should stay crisp for 2 weeks.

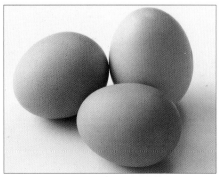

**Per Portion** Energy 410kcal/1737kJ; Protein 4.3g; Carbohydrate 95.2g, of which sugars 27.7g; Fat 3.1g, of which saturates 0.8g; Cholesterol 99mg; Calcium 45mg; Fibre 0.7g; Sodium 59mg.

# SPICE ISLAND ICE CREAM

*WITH SUCH A RANGE OF TROPICAL FRUIT AND SPICES, THERE IS ALMOST NO LIMIT TO THE FLAVOURS OF INDONESIAN ICE CREAM. IN THIS DELICIOUS DESSERT, WARMING SPICES ARE COMBINED WITH COOL, SMOOTH AND RICH ICE CREAM TO MAKE A TRULY MEMORABLE, AND VERY INDONESIAN, DESSERT.*

SERVES SIX

INGREDIENTS
500ml/17fl oz/2 cups double
   (heavy) cream
6–8 cloves
6–8 cardamom seeds
3–4 star anise
3 cinnamon sticks
90g/3½oz/½ cup caster
   (superfine) sugar
150ml/¼ pint/⅔ cup water
4 large (US extra large) eggs
ground cinnamon or nutmeg,
   to decorate

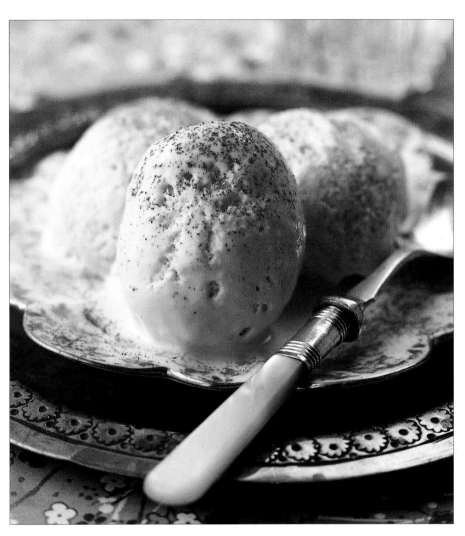

**1** In a heavy pan, heat the cream with the spices until scalding. Remove the pan from the heat and leave the cream to infuse (steep) until cool.

**2** In a separate pan, heat the sugar and water together, stirring all the time, until the sugar has dissolved. Bring to the boil and boil for 2–3 minutes without stirring, then lower the heat and simmer for 5 minutes. Remove from the heat and leave to cool for 10 minutes.

**3** Whisk the eggs together in a bowl. Gradually trickle in the hot syrup, whisking all the time, until the mixture becomes light and airy like a mousse. Strain the spice-infused cream into the mixture and whisk well together until thoroughly blended.

**4** Pour the mixture into an ice cream maker and churn until frozen, according to the manufacturer's instructions. Alternatively, pour into a freezer-proof container and freeze, uncovered, for 1–2 hours until beginning to set around the edges. Turn into a bowl and beat to break up the ice crystals. Return to the freezer container, freeze and beat again, then cover and freeze until firm.

**5** Decorate with a sprinkling of cinnamon and serve.

**COOK'S TIP**
This ice cream is very good served with warm apple or pear tart, or with flambéed bananas.

**Per Portion** Energy 522kcal/2157kJ; Protein 5.6g; Carbohydrate 17.1g, of which sugars 17.1g; Fat 48.5g, of which saturates 28.9g; Cholesterol 241mg; Calcium 68mg; Fibre 0g; Sodium 66mg.

# AVOCADO JUICE

*One of many unusual sweet delights found at street stalls in Indonesia and the Philippines is this thick, syrupy avocado juice, which falls somewhere between a snack and a drink. Once again, the South-east Asian passion for condensed milk defines this drink. Mix the delectable avocado purée into the sweet milk and enjoy at your leisure.*

SERVES TWO

INGREDIENTS
    30ml/2 tbsp sugar
    30ml/2 tbsp water
    2 ripe avocados
    a handful of ice cubes or
        crushed ice
    30ml/2 tbsp sweetened
        condensed milk

**1** Put the sugar and water in a heavy pan and heat gently, stirring all the time, until the sugar has dissolved. Bring to the boil without stirring, then remove from the heat and leave to cool.

**COOK'S TIP**
As with any recipe that calls for them, use only properly ripened, seasonal avocados, as those available 'year round' do not have enough flavour.

**2** When the sugar syrup is cold, put the flesh of the avocados in a large bowl or food processor, add the cooled sugar syrup and mash or blend until smooth.

**3** Put the ice cubes into two tall glasses, spoon in the avocado mixture, then drizzle the condensed milk over the top. Serve immediately, with a long spoon, so that the drinkers can mix the avocado with the condensed milk at their leisure.

**Per Portion** 324kcal/1353kJ; Protein 3.9g; Carbohydrate 30.1g, of which sugars 28.7g; Fat 21.6g, of which saturates 5.5g; Cholesterol 8mg; Calcium 84mg; Fibre 3.4g; Sodium 39mg.

# FRESH GINGER TEA

*GINGER TEA IS A SPECIALITY OF THE HIGH-ALTITUDE REGIONS OF INDONESIA. OFTEN YOU WILL FIND AN OLD WOMAN MAKING THE TEA IN THE SMALL HILL SHELTERS MADE OF BAMBOO, WHERE PEOPLE STOP TO REST AND DRINK A GLASS OF THIS HOT AND SPICY BREW. IT IS ALSO ENJOYED AS A BREAKFAST, AS IT IS WARMING AND STIMULATES THE DIGESTION.*

SERVES FOUR

INGREDIENTS

1 litre/1¾ pints/4 cups water
40g/1½oz fresh root ginger, peeled
  and sliced
1–2 cinnamon sticks
5ml/1 tsp black peppercorns
30ml/2 tbsp palm sugar (jaggery)
115g/4oz/¾ cup coconut flesh,
  finely shredded

**COOK'S TIP**
The tea improves with standing, so, if convenient, you can make it in advance and reheat it before serving.

**1** Bring the water, ginger, cinnamon sticks, peppercorns and sugar to the boil in a pan, stirring until the sugar has dissolved. Boil rapidly for 2 minutes, then simmer for at least 15 minutes.

**2** Divide the shredded coconut between four heatproof glasses and strain the hot ginger tea into the glasses. Serve immediately, with a spoon to scoop up the coconut.

**Per Portion** Energy 120kcal/500kJ; Protein 0.9g; Carbohydrate 8.8g, of which sugars 8.8g; Fat 9.3g, of which saturates 8g; Cholesterol 0mg; Calcium 8mg; Fibre 2.1g; Sodium 5mg.

# INDEX